THE THREE-LEGGED STOOL

Relationships First—Success Follows

THE THREE-LEGGED STOOL

Relationships First—Success Follows

Roland S. Boreham, Jr.

Rutledge Books, Inc. Danbury, CT

Copyright © 1998 by Roland S. Boreham, Jr.

ALL RIGHTS RESERVED
Rutledge Books, Inc.
107 Mill Plain Road, Danbury, CT 06811
1-800-278-8533

Manufactured in the United States of America

Cataloging in Publication Data
Boreham, Jr., Roland S.
    The three legged stool: relationships first — success follows

    ISBN: 1-58244-016-6

    1. Industrial management. 2. Creative ability in business.

658

TABLE OF CONTENTS

PREFACE

For years I have been preaching a message about the importance of good relationships to business success. And I have often been frustrated with the growing tendency I see among many managers, particularly newly minted MBAs, who want to think only about numbers, cost controls, and financial analyses. I have railed against this problem for so many years and to so many audiences that I have finally decided to follow the advice of many of my colleagues who have said, "Rollie, you really ought to write a book about it." Perhaps they were just trying to shut me up, thinking that if I were writing about it, I would quit talking about it continually. But I haven't quit talking about it, and now I am writing about it.

This book is about the important, and too often ignored, human side of corporate success. It is a book that hopes to convince the reader that the most important thing you can do as a manager of any business is to build strong, long-lasting relationships — relationships with customers, employees and owners. It isn't a touchy-feely book that talks about how to court, flatter, and personally endear yourself to these constituencies. But it is about building up good relationships through long-term commitments to fairness, good communication, the building of trust, and the pursuit of win-win strategies.

As you might already guess, the ideas here do not emphasize the quantitative approach — the crunching of numbers road to profits. I was educated first as a physicist and later as an engineer, so I do firmly believe that numbers have an important role to play in business. But I don't believe that numbers, bottom lines, and financial analyses should be the sole, or even major, consideration in corporate decision-making and, particularly, in corporate success.

Most of the ideas and examples I present in this book have come to me over a forty-five-year career, beginning as an independent sales representative, and eventually becoming the CEO and Chairman, for a company manufacturing electric motors and drives, Baldor Electric. Baldor is a publicly held company employing about 4,000 people. Although my personal experience in this specific business is the environment which helped me form these ideas, I think the approach I suggest is applicable to any business of any size.

THE THREE-LEGGED STOOL

Good Relationships Lead To Good Profits

Too often heard in the hallways and meeting rooms of American businesses is a dialogue that goes something like this: "If we could only get our numbers looking better, we could take better care of our employees. And we could be more generous with the shareholders. Several of them are asking for better returns on their investment. But first we have to get better profits." The dialogue often continues with, "I know we need to take better care of our customers, but first we have to make some money."

Wrong! It just doesn't work that way! First, you must take care of your employees, shareholders, and customers. First, you must build strong, long-lasting relationships with these three groups. Then, profits will follow. Or as my father told me and my brothers many times, "First, you've got to do a good job at whatever you're doing, then you'll end up making money. Don't start out just thinking about making money."

The premise of this book is that good relationships lead to good profits. You may accept this as a truism (if you do, I believe you are in the minority) or I may need to do a bit of convincing. To begin to try to convince you of the truth of this statement, I suggest you think about an analogous situation in education, the connection between learning and good grades. All of us have been students and found ourselves in this situation. Anyone who has done any teaching in which students are graded has had a student come to them and say he is very interested in knowing what the course is about and in learning as much as possible. The student may be motivated by a pure desire to learn or because the subject is of interest to him or is a part of his major. Compare this type of student to the one that says, "What do I need to do to get a good grade in this course?" Which student do you think will learn the most? And which student, in the long run, will make the best grades?

A student concerned only about a grade is like a company concerned only about profits. In both cases, this is short-term thinking and this makes success more difficult. Just as the student must focus on learning, the company must focus on building relationships. Just as grades follow learning, profits follow strong relationships.

Good Relationships With Whom

There are three constituencies who can make or break any business, whether it is a small six-table restaurant or a large corporation. These are the customers, the employees, and the owners. In this book I often refer to shareholders. Shareholders are owners. I believe my ideas are applicable whether those who run the business are the sole shareholders (owners of small businesses), partial owners, or non-owners.

True, there are other constituencies that are important to any business, such as suppliers, government agencies, regulatory or quasi-governmental groups, and the community. In fact, suppliers have become so important that I have devoted a chapter to them. Although these other constituencies are important and cannot be ignored, they are not as vital to the "life and death" of a company as the first three. I often use the image of a business as a three-legged stool, with each of the three major constituencies—customers, employees, and shareholders—being represented by one of the legs.

For many years I have been an active member of the American Business Conference, a coalition of growth companies concerned with governmental policies. A few years ago I and a couple of my fellow members of the American Business Conference were in Washington having lunch with two prominent senators. One of them was complaining rather bitterly about his constituents. He said that sometimes he felt forced to do things he didn't particularly want to do and to vote in ways he didn't want to vote because he felt that otherwise he could lose his constituents' support and, therefore, would no longer be his state's representative in the Senate. He seemed to be appealing to us businessmen for sympathy. I had just read a statement by William Simon indicationg that a customer order to a business is equal to a vote to a politician. On that basis, I ventured cautiously to tell this gentleman that we ran for election every day. In other words, we need these votes to stay in business. If we don't get them, no matter how good our product, our technology, our organization, our manufacturing methods, we won't survive.

One of the senators got a little huffy about this, but the other one understood very well what we meant. He was a very fortunate combination of a public servant who understood free enterprise and also has a big heart (a really winning combination). He said he never thought of it this way, but that point of view made a lot of sense.

And also just to kind of "load it on" we brought up the fact that we had three constituencies that could make or break us. Not only the customer group, who certainly has that power, but also employees and shareholders. The employee who continues to do his job for the company is voting. The shareholder who continues to hold or increase his investment in the company is voting. And the customer who continues to buy the company's product is voting.

This book emphasizes the importance of good relationships with these three key constituencies and discusses how to develop these good relationships with them. It focuses on the way we treat others and the way they treat us. Success is a matter of how well we conduct our relationships with other people and in our transactions with other people and groups of people.

The message that businesses must focus on relationships with constituencies should not lull you into thinking that you don't have to concern yourself with making a profit. Obviously every business must be concerned with profit. It is just the point of this book that profit should not be the primary focus of business planning and strategies. If you are worrying too much about making a profit, you very likely won't. If you worry about how to build up good, strong, long-lasting relationships with your business's constituencies, profits will follow.

Relationships And Mission Statements

The great business guru, Peter Drucker, often said that the first step is to know who we are and what we are and just as important, who we want to be and what we want to be. In other words, what's our mission? Once we have decided that, the next step is to start from the very beginning to build good relationships with customers, employees, and shareholders.

What constitutes a good mission statement? Good ones are like good commencement addresses: scarce and short. And the best ones are definitely "relationship" oriented. The one that I helped to write for Baldor Electric, and one in which I continue to take great pride, is just twenty-one words.

Our mission is: To be the best (as determined by our customers) marketers,   designers and manufacturers of electric motors and drives.

Baldor's mission statement has three supporting sentences stating how to achieve the mission and emphasizing the importance of the business's key constituencies.

1. Provide better value to our customers than any of our competitors.
2. Attract and retain competent employees dedicated to reaching our goals and objectives.
3. Produce good long-term results for our shareholders.

Not An Either-Or Situation

Recently on a radio business show, a professor was discussing the problem the Chinese were facing in developing their economy. A major problem, according to the professor, was that businesses in the past, under the communistic system, only concerned themselves with keeping people employed. Their major concern was providing jobs. The professor contrasted this with the new capitalistic China and said that now the major concern is making a profit.

The discussion presented these as two opposites—providing jobs or making a profit. The growing economy of China was dependent upon a complete shift in thinking, according to the professor. The person responsible for business in China must quit worrying about providing jobs for workers and must begin to focus on the bottom line.

It may go a bit too far to suggest that the businesses in communistic China were focusing only on building strong relationships with employees. But I do think some wisdom can be gained from this radio discussion. I propose that focusing first and foremost on the bottom line, making a profit, is not what leads to success in entrepreneurial, capitalistic systems. In fact, concerning oneself only with making a profit may very well decrease or eliminate the possibility of making one. Rather, the focus must be on building strong relationships with three constituencies—including worrying about relationships with employees—providing them with stable jobs with good wages and working conditions, treating them as important members of the business team, and providing them with opportunities to make real contributions.

So I think this business professor was wrong in his basic assumptions. I don't think the road to success for Chinese businesses is to quit worrying about providing jobs and start worrying about bottom lines. It is not an either-or situation.

Balance And Flexibility

To be successful, good relationships with all three constituencies are important and there needs to be *balance* among the three. It is useful to think about the three constituencies as a three-legged stool, as I mentioned earlier. If one leg is weak or is not the same length as the others, the sitter who depends upon it will end up on his backside. The company that doesn't equally emphasize the three constituencies will end up on its backside—and perhaps in bankruptcy.

Favoring one constituency over the other simply doesn't work. Many companies have found this out. If one looks back through the history of American businesses many examples can be found of companies that were good at one or even two of these three relationships, but failed on the third and, therefore, failed in total. Some of the greatest manufacturers of products in the United States no longer exist because of this failure.

The automobile industry is a good example of this. Prior to World War II, the finest automobiles in the United States were made by the Packard Motor Company. What is now considered to be the top luxury car was second choice then. In the middle and lower price range, people who really knew automobiles often voted for the Studebaker as being the best product, the most durable, and best performing. These two companies were known for superior quality.

Packard Motor Company made a superb Rolls Royce V-12 aircraft engine during World War II. It was a far better product than the equivalent engine made by the largest auto manufacturer. Both engines were rated at about the same horsepower and were about the same weight, but the Packard Rolls Royce far outperformed the other. It was not only higher performing but it was more durable.

Perhaps people at Packard believed, as did many others, the old maxim, "Build a better mousetrap and they will beat a path to your door." Wrong! This old expression has probably caused the demise of more manufacturers and businesses than even, "The customer is always right."

Studebaker made the best aircraft 50-caliber machine guns. The other two manufacturers were the government arsenal at Springfield and a division of the largest motor car company. The savvy old tech sergeants and master sergeants would tell from the serial numbers which machine guns were built by which of the manufacturers. The Studebakers were always grabbed first.

The point being made by these examples is that if quality ("better mousetraps") were the hallmark of success—if having the best product automatically leads to good profits—why aren't these two fine companies still in business and still making automobiles? The answer is that they didn't have balance and strong relationships with their three key constituencies. Their dealer networks were weak and customer relationships suffered.

Another concept that is important, possibly even equally important as balance, is flexibility. Businesses need to have the ability to adapt to new environments. I believe it was Socrates in one of Plato's writings who said that intelligence is the ability to adapt. Flexibility is vital to building and maintaining good long-term relationships due to inevitable changes in the needs and wants of these constituencies. At the same time, and it sometimes appears to be contradictory, customers, employees, and owners have a desire for consistency. Predictability is important. Balance, flexibility, and predictability—maintaining these simultaneously is certainly a challenge.

Pricing And Balancing Relationships

How can the company be fair to the customer, show a fair profit to the owners/shareholders and generate enough cash flow to treat employees fairly? The answer to that question is, "That's the name of the game." It is not easy. If it were, everyone would do it. It requires thought, experience, and constant checking and double-checking with each one of the constituencies to see if they feel they are being treated well.

The pricing policies of a company tell a lot about the company itself. And they tell a lot about the balance a company manages among its constituencies. If they are biased toward either the owner/shareholder, the employee, or the customer, this bias will be seen. Many times companies don't even realize they do this, but the customers, shareholders/owners, and employees do.

Many years ago Al Capp, the creator of the great social commentary comic strip, *Lil Abner*, drew a character, General Bullmoose. General Bullmoose would often proudly say, "What's good for General Bullmoose is good for the country." This was back in the 1950s and most everyone knew that General Bullmoose was a parody of the leadership of General Motors. This showed the bias that was probably there: towards what is good for the shareholders of General Motors is good for everyone. With 40 or 50 percent of market share back then, who would say that General Motors was not taking care of its customers or employees? It took many years to show. The larger the object, the more the momentum. In the 1960s and 1970s, this lack of attention to customers and employees began to show. Market share started shrinking and employee relations, which were never really cordial, deteriorated further.

How manufacturers or service providers price their products has always been a subject of debate and controversy. It probably always will be. There are several different pricing methods, and most of them do not help build good relationships. In fact, in many cases they are destructive to good relationships. Let's examine some of these and how they effect relationships.

One form of pricing policy is known commonly as the profit maximization model. Does this mean the maximizing of margins or maximizing the total results of sales times margin? If so, what assumptions are made about the relationship between price, sales volume, and total profits? This is always a difficult subject. And does this theory take human relationships into account? Probably not!

Another form of pricing policy is following the competition. This is the simplest pricing strategy, but it brings up some interesting questions, such as, "What if the competition is going down the wrong road?" or "What are they doing which is good for their customers, employees, and shareholders?" This might not be good for your three constituencies. In fact, it would be a coincidence if it were good for both of the companies, particularly if one is much larger or has a different corporate culture.

We had an interesting example of the problems of following the competition when we followed the largest company in our industry on pricing fractional horsepower and integral horsepower DC motors. Our competitor had two different divisions supplying these two different products. One division was very aggressive and was a low-cost producer, pricing the product accordingly. The other division was the opposite. There was a huge discontinuity between the prices of the two divisions. When we and the other motor manufacturers followed, we looked foolish. We decided to break away. We were the only competitor who took on a new policy which we called "sensible pricing." At first we were called mavericks, nonconformists, and oddballs. However, we stuck to our guns and, after several years, we were successful in gaining better relationships with customers. We gained market share. Profits also improved. Was it a coincidence that profits improved? No, for when relationships improve, profits improve.

One of the things we found with this "sensible pricing" policy was that we greatly improved our relationships with our salespeople, as well as our customers. We reconfirmed an old theory about marketing, namely, that any marketing policy that puts your salesmen in a position where they can't give a logical reason to the customers for the policy is damaging. Or to put it in other terms, when you put your salespeople in a bad position, you put the whole company in a bad position. This damages relationships not only with the customers but with the salespeople, who, of course, are the direct link between the company and the customer.

Cost plus pricing is an old method used for years, particularly in government contracting. It reminds me of the old joke from World War II where three industrialists were having an expensive luncheon. At the conclusion of lunch, all three grabbed for the check. The first industrialist said to let him have the check because, "I'm in the 80 percent tax bracket, so this lunch will only cost my company 20 percent of the tab." The second said, "I am in the excess profit category, so the lunch won't cost my company a nickel." The third one quickly took the check and walked to the cashier saying, "I'll take care of this because I am on a cost plus contract, and I'll make money on this lunch."

At Baldor, we follow a value pricing theory. I think this is a sensible pricing policy. We and others proved many years ago that value is "in the eyes of the customers." It is the customer's perception that counts. Value is proportional directly to quality (as perceived by customers) and service (as perceived by customers) and inversely related to cost (price) and time (availability). These four variables form the core of the Baldor Value Formula, which will be discussed at some length in the next chapter.

This theory of pricing comes close to what might be called relational pricing. When value for the customers is taken into account, including what is best for the employees and the shareholders, we are getting right down to what is best for overall relationships.

To the inexperienced business person, the word "competitive" often means being the lowest priced. There are some good cartoons drawn showing the man who was always the lowest bidder. He usually has holes in his shoes and patches on his trousers. The term "competitive" to experienced people means being somewhere in the ballpark. Another way of saying it is a fair price and a consistent one. It must be consistent or the regular buyer feels that he is being "lowballed." Low balling is the practice of coming in low with the intention of gradually raising the price up on a preplanned basis after the customer comes to depend on the company producing the product or service. To most, this is considered unethical. It is practiced by amateurs, both domestic and foreign. It is not good relationship selling, nor relationship building.

The CEO

One day as I was talking with a good friend about the ideas in this book, it occurred to us that the first letters of the major constituencies—customers, employees and owners—formed the acronym CEO. We liked that and found it symbolic. The successful business is one with strong and good relationships with its CEOs!

Isn't that a great way to remember? So the next three chapters tell how to build positive relationships with customers, employees, and owners.

CUSTOMERS

Introduction

A company must build strong relationships with its customers, employees and owners. It is these relationships that will lead to a company's success. This chapter will focus in more detail on the importance of these customer relationships and try to give ideas as to how to develop these good relationships.

Customers are people. They want to be treated right. They want to feel safe and secure in doing business with the supplier. They want to feel that they are treated as important people. Also, they want to feel they have made a good decision in picking the supplier in the first place.

Sounds pretty obvious, doesn't it? But it's not so obvious to some. Just observe the way that many businesses refer to customers. First, they give them a number (kind of similar to prison). Then, they keep track of other numbers such as dollar sales, accounts receivable, numbers about how many days for payment terms, prices, etc. All numbers!

Therefore, it is absolutely inevitable that unless management teaches, educates, convinces, and maybe even cajoles the employees into thinking of customers as people, most will not do it. They will think of them as numbers since in many companies that is all they will see or hear. Okay, first I hope we agree that we must think of customers as people and we must think of them as people who have their own perspective. Perception by the customer is what really counts. Even if the perception is based on few, or incomplete, facts, it determines what the customer thinks. This, in turn, affects his actions, including what and where he buys.

Same with relationships. What the customer thinks is a good, strong relationship becomes one, unless the supplier fails to reciprocate. Once the relationship becomes good and strong, it is very unlikely that the supplier's competitors will be able to capture this customer's business, unless neglected.

Even strong and secure relationships must be nurtured. To do this they must be recognized as being valuable and treated accordingly. Neglect or "taking for granted" can gradually undermine even the best of relationships.

Mission-Customer Connection

As an experiment, try sometime walking into a manufacturing plant, a retail store, or even a non-profit building like a library or hospital, and ask, "What are we doing here?" or more accurately, "What is the mission of this organization?" This is a form of a test, and often a very revealing one. If the people responding don't use the word "customer" or "patient" or "client" in the first sentence or two, chances are it is not a very successful organization.

One of my favorite entrepreneurs of all time ran a nonprofit organization. I know that is an unusual combination, which made him an even more noteworthy person. He ran the largest hospital in our town and, in my opinion, the best one. By "best", I mean from the point of view of the customers, i.e., the patients.

He was always teaching or, some said, "preaching." One of his favorite maneuvers was to prowl the halls of this hospital and whenever he encountered a new employee he would accost them with some quick question. One of his favorite questions was, "Who is the most important person in this hospital?" Sometimes employees would answer, "You, Mr. Altman." When he said wrong on that one, it was often followed by answers such as the doctors or even the trustees. He would sometimes straighten them out although sometimes he would just say, "Wrong." Either way the new employees soon found out that the correct answer was "the patients." He made this point over and over. Some of the doctors didn't always agree. We patients almost always did.

To sum up, as a smart man once said, "I don't believe the customer is always right but he is always the customer." Or as another said, "The customer is the reason we are here."

Customers Are Important/Show Them
How do we get everyone to think of customers as people, important people? One of the best ways to help this happen is to encourage customers to visit. Show them off. Give them "hero medals" (not just name tags), with big streamers that say the magic word "customer". Then the corollary to this is to visit customers yourself. Not just the salesman assigned to that customer

but also the bosses and people from the factory floor.

Some people resist this idea by saying that some people are important and some are not. So how can you treat them all as if they are important? The rejoinder to this is that everyone is important in one way or another. In the case of a customer's organization, one must at least believe that each of the customer's people is important or they wouldn't be there in the first place. Sometimes the ones that look least important are actually vital to the success of that company. Often this isn't apparent until one becomes much better acquainted.

Many examples of this important principle come to mind, and one in particular. This was a case where a very successful organization, growing rapidly, was a very important potential customer of ours. Unfortunately, at the time, our competitor had the lion's share of the business and we had a small part. One time we had an appointment for lunch with the manager of this firm, but the president of their largest supplier showed up unannounced and took the manager and his entire staff out to lunch. There we were, thinking we had an appointment, instead left standing around with nothing to do. Upon looking around we noticed that one staff member was still there and hadn't gone with the rest of them.

We met this young man and asked him why. He said, "I wasn't invited." So we invited him to lunch and found out that he was a new salesman on the staff. He had just arrived from out of state, didn't know anyone, and was even thinking about going home.

After some discussion we found this young man had a great deal of knowledge of the markets we were serving and some knowledge of our products, to which we added more. He was such a capable person that within two or three years he rose to the top of that corporation.

He never mentioned our having taken him to lunch that day when he had been left behind, or the knowledge of our products which we had the opportunity to convey to him that day, but we gradually became the leading supplier to his company. Was that because we did a better job, or because the competitor slipped, or because we treated him like an important person? Or was it all three?

Knowing And Taking Care Of Customers

If your company knows more about customers than your competitors, you have a tremendous competitive advantage. Also, more knowledge almost always leads to better relationships. If other factors are equal or even nearly equal, the seller or supplier with the superior knowledge of the customer and with the better relationship will win nine out of ten times.

If this is the case, and our tests and experience show that it is, why isn't this discussed more often? Is it due to the subjectivity of this issue? Or to put it in other words, is it due to the difficulty of reducing this to numerical analysis?

There have been many books written about Sam Walton, including one by Sam himself. Everyone seems to have a different theory about why he was such a big success. I know one reason. I saw it many times myself. He was an absolute fanatic about taking care of customers.

"Taking care of customers" is more than just giving them good service and treating them well. It means crawling right into their heads and finding out what they want and what they need. Sam was a real expert at this. The best I've even seen. One of the reasons he was so good at it was that he worked at it. Even on social occasions he would buttonhole customers or even prospective customers and ask them what they wanted to buy, what they found that they liked, what didn't they find that they needed and what might be put into stock; also what they liked or didn't like about the stores themselves.

I remember one night at a social occasion he asked one of the ladies present (he talked to ladies about these things more than men because he recognized they were more frequent customers) which of the two stores in her town did she think was the best. When she answered, he seemed surprised, as she picked the store that did less volume than one of his pet stores. He pursued this and wanted to know why she preferred one over the other. When she said it was a matter of ease of access, he whipped a piece of paper out of his pocket and wrote this down.

Guess what? Within a couple of days another driveway had been added to the store in question. It was not a month or two later; it was a day or two later.

Just as you must know your customers, you must also know those who compete with you for that customer's business. Another Sam Walton story highlights his devotion to this. A Wal-Mart associate told me about a time Sam himself arrived to pick up him and some other directors at an airport about 50 or 60 miles away from their company headquarters. Sam arrived on a bus, and shortly after leaving the airport, he got on a microphone and told them they had a little extra time, and that on the way to headquarters for their meeting, they were going to stop at a couple of their retail stores and also a competitor's store.

Much to everyone's amazement, he directed the driver to pull into a competitor's store parking lot. First, he asked the directors to observe how few cars were in this parking lot, compared to the Wal-Mart. Then to their further amazement, he led them right into the competitor's store. He showed them how the aisles were not as wide as they should be, how some of the merchandise was not well displayed, and other shortcomings of the store. Actually, the way I heard the story wasn't so much that he "knocked" the competitor, but that he wanted them to see a contrast between the way his competitor operated and the better and more efficient ways that the Wal-Mart stores operated. Naturally, some of them were apprehensive that they would be "thrown out," but even though Sam was recognized, there were no unpleasant incidents. The fact is that Sam got his point across, pointing out many competitive advantages held by Wal-Mart.

When they arrived at a Wal-Mart, Sam pointed out another competitive advantage to his director. The salespeople at Wal-Mart greeted everyone. Also, a few questions showed that the sales staff was more knowledgeable about the merchandise than had been those at the competitor's store.

The Sales Staff:

The Company's Primary Link To Customers

Everyone in the company must work to build strong relationships with customers. But particularly in businesses where salespeople go out to see customers, what factors are possibly more important to the customer's appraisal of the company's worth than the customer's appraisal of the salesperson's worth. I think all of us manufacturers and wholesalers have had the experience that as we go around to different territories, we find that in some territories our companies are very well thought of, respected and trusted, while in other territories we are not so respected, trusted or well thought of. How can this be? We are supplying the same services and/or manufacturing the same products for the areas where we are well thought of as the areas where we are not. How can the reason for this be other than the quality of the salespeople as perceived by the customer?

Several years ago I had a very noteworthy experience illustrating this important point. In studying competitors, which of course is an important subject for any business (but not as important as studying customers), we found over and over that one competitor was not doing too well and was not well thought of by customers in the East or North or the West. Paradoxically, however, they appeared to be quite well thought of throughout the South, all the way from Memphis to Atlanta to Richmond to Tampa to New Orleans.

The only factor that we could possibly think of to explain this difference was salespeople. Therefore, we investigated who this company had doing their selling in the South. (In other words, we followed the idea of not studying what went wrong, but with the theory that you learn more by studying what is right.) We kept being referred to a certain person both by the customers in the South and the salespeople who reported to this regional manager.

Curiosity, plus a bit of greed, I must confess, led us to meet this man. Within the first few minutes of the meeting, we found some of the reasons for this mystery. He was not only a very knowledgeable person, but he had a great amount of enthusiasm and love for what he was doing. We got along so well that we induced him to come join our company. He did a good job for us for the next 15 years until he retired.

Knowing the importance of the sales staff to the success of the company, why do so many companies cut sales staff at the first sign of storm clouds on the horizon? Shouldn't they sometimes do the opposite? In an epidemic of large company downsizings, some of the most vicious and widespread downsizing has been among sales organizations.

One reason for this, of course, is the new technology of computers talking to computers and EDI (Electronic Data Interchange) as well as telemarketing, being planned, or at least hoped, to substitute, or partially substitute for salespeople talking to customers face-to-face. More will be said about the role of technology later in this chapter.

When only one side of the coin is examined, namely the expense side rather than the revenue side, these new technologies can be very appealing. Recruiting salespeople, training them, and sorting out the ones that have the talent, ambition, and drive to really take good care of customers from the ones that don't, is an expensive proposition. This is particularly true when companies need to put salespeople "on the road." Traveling expenses are much higher than they were a few years ago. In fact, with the possible exception of health care, travel expense ranks near the highest inflation factor of all business expenses.

What this all adds up to is the need for recognition that salespeople are vital to the success of any company, regardless of whether they are selling a product or a service. Also, this is true regardless of whether they are in the retail business where customers come to them or in wholesale or manufacturing where salespeople need to go to the customer.

Perhaps one of the best illustrations of the importance of good salespeople is an examination of successful small businesses. Many small businesses, whether they be service or manufacturing, often have the owner or the boss being the "chief salesman." Is this because the small businessperson has a better understanding of what is vitally important to make a business grow and prosper? Or is this due to the difficulty of securing good salespeople? Or is it the strong desire of most successful small business owners to find out more, firsthand, about their customers' needs and wants? And it isn't only small businesses where the owner-boss is the chief salesman. Isn't Bill Gates the top salesperson for Microsoft?

No doubt about it, really good salespeople, whether retail, wholesale or manufacturing, are scarce. Some say they are born, some say they are made, some say it is a combination of the two. No doubt about it, sales training is a very important subject in any company. This is particularly true as a company grows.

Ask Questions To Build Relationships

I recall an experience working with an "old pro" salesman. We had a situation where this customer really needed what we were selling and logically should have been buying from us. This is most frustrating for salespeople when they know that they have the right combination, yet are somehow not able to plug it together. We talked to just about everyone in the company except the "big man." He was usually quite inaccessible. We finally persisted and his assistant told us we could have "just five minutes." We took it. We were then warned again in the outer office by his secretary (one of those queen bees who looked like she had been there a hundred years) that we had "just five minutes" with Mr. Big. We got the point.

What happened was really amazing. Even though I have seen it several times since, it still amazes me. Mr. Big greeted us rather coolly. He was obviously very busy. His body language and words both told us this quite clearly.

Then after he used about two of our five minutes telling us how busy he was, he asked us what he could do for us. My old pro associate asked a few good questions. I say "good questions" because he had obviously done his homework. He had read their annual reports, their quarterly reports, their product catalogs. I believe he had even read their 10-Ks and 10-Qs. Mr. Big seemed to warm up after a while and indicated this by saying something to the effect that, "You seem to know a lot about our company." The response was, "Yes, we do, and we think that we can have a good future together."

After some more questions and some more answers, Mr. Big gradually warmed. His answers were getting longer and more descriptive. Then about 45 minutes later he asked us if we would like to see the plant and look around the company.

It is always a real pleasure to walk out past the secretary and the assistant with Mr. Big being quite friendly and effusive. Then his asking if we wanted to leave our things there and look around the plant and then stay and have lunch with him? To one who has worked with salespeople of many types, big ones and little ones, good ones and not so good ones, on big deals and little deals, and who has worked in sales training for many years, this is a thing of beauty to behold.

Back to relationships, one could well ask, "How about your relationships with Mr. Big's assistants?" Good question. Answer: go back and rebuild from the ground up at first opportunity. Then tie this in with your new and good relationship at the top.

I have been working with professional salespeople for many years. I have often been asked what's the most significant difference between professional salespeople and amateurs. It is a good question, as often the amateur seems to know his products pretty well, seems to be presentable, usually uses good grammar, but somehow doesn't get the job done—the job being defined as bringing in good, steady, high-quality business to his principal.

The difference that I have noticed over and over, working with hundreds of salespeople over many years, is that the professionals *ask* and the amateurs *tell*. Too much sales training, both academic and company-sponsored, is spent in preparing presentations and practicing how to deliver them. Often presentations have a negative value. For one thing, unless many questions have been asked ahead of time, how does one know that the presentation is on target as to what the customer needs and wants? Often it is not. The only place where presentations really pay off is after the completion of a thorough assessment of what the customer needs and wants. This is accomplished by asking many questions, then listening to the answers and testing them.

Several years ago, when I was young and inexperienced, I worked with one of the greatest salesmen that I have ever had the pleasure to know. Cal was not an educated man, nor was he known as being brilliant or quick or "fast on his feet," but he was intelligent, knowledgeable and always very effective. He consistently got the job done.

As a neophyte I studied him with the goal of trying to find out why he was so successful when many others weren't. The reasons weren't very apparent at first. After a while I noticed his characteristic of asking not only a lot of questions, but good questions. Also, he had a way of asking these questions that did not offend the customer. I saw several times that people who I thought were "tough guys" responded to his questions, answered them cheerfully, and almost eagerly waited to see where he was headed with the next question.

One time we had a particularly tough situation where we were attempting to secure approval of our product from a major oil company. We had already spent time with their purchasing people, engineering people, and administrators. We had asked a lot of questions and responded, showing that we had what they wanted and what they needed. But still no results. This finally culminated in a meeting in one of those "big company" boardrooms with the long, mahogany table down the center, highly polished, surrounded by some highly polished, big company people. Cal started out by asking some more questions and then showing these gentlemen that we had responded and had come up with the product that fit what they needed and what they had been asking for. Still no action. Still not much response from these big company people.

Finally, there came that "awkward pause" which most people dread. Of course, most experienced people know that these pauses can be very useful, even though they are uncomfortable. Cal let this pause go on. I had a feeling he transmitted somehow to me, "If you open your mouth, I will break your neck." So I didn't. Finally, the long, it seemed like minutes, pause was broken by Cal saying loudly and even a bit crudely, "Well, how about it?" The responders came right up out of their chairs, as I did, and they came down saying, "Well, yes. I guess we can work this out."

Listen To Build Good Relationships

There is a great story, supposedly true, that Franklin Delano Roosevelt complained many times during his governorship of New York and after a couple of terms as president, that he had shaken hands with thousands and thousands of people in reception lines. He also complained that everybody seemed to say what was expected to be said and didn't really do much listening. He contended their brains were only concerned with what they were going to say or what impression they were making. They were not listening.

Being a puckish man at times and also not above trying an experiment, one night in the reception line he just kept smiling and saying, "I murdered my aunt this morning." People would just smile and say, "That's nice, " or "Lovely to see you" or even "Beautiful evening." Finally a good listener came along. He gave the president a sharp look and said, "I'm sure she had it coming to her."

To improve relationships with customers, as with anyone we know, including friends and family, we need to listen well. Many books have been written about listening, so I am not going to duplicate them here, except to add one thought. This thought is, "Listen to *what*?" Listen to the answers to all the questions you ask. And you should ask lots of good questions.

Knowing A Cutomer's Wants And Needs

One of the most difficult things about establishing and improving relationships with customers is that, as the old-timers know, it is not enough to satisfy them, as some of the quality gurus say. What kind of relationship would we have if we only satisfied the customer and our competitor did better than that? Where would we be? Probably out in the parking lot.

Another way to look at it is that all customers, large or small, have both needs and wants. Unfortunately (or fortunately if you are able to bring them together and the competitor can't), the two are usually somewhat separate. A classical example is the old saying about the man with the champagne appetite and the beer pocketbook.

Customers, even sophisticated ones, often need a product of a certain performance level but want a product of considerably higher performance. Then, to further complicate it, they want to pay the price of the lower performance and secure the higher.

Or to put it in other terms, we engineers are often not good salespeople; the reason being that we concentrate on the needs and often do a very good job of it. However, unless we find out what the customer wants, and it is often different, we can be in the position of "winning the argument and losing the customer."

Oppositely, if we have a person contacting that customer who is very good at understanding the wants but doesn't understand the needs—that relationship is a short one. This person is sometimes referred to as the "Willie Loman" type. The relationship will start out "happy", but once the customer finds out we aren't filling his real needs, he will go to where his needs will be filled. In other words, the engineering-type salespeople who fills the needs but not the wants doesn't get the order in the first place. The more empathetic type of salespeople who understands the wants, but not the needs, will get a couple of orders but eventually lose the customer.

"Before" picture shows needs and wants separated and the product or service in a third position. For a good satisfactory long-term relationship with the customer it is important that the three be brought

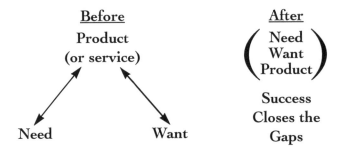

Before

Product
(or service)

After

(Need
Want
Product)

**Success
Closes the
Gaps**

close together. How to do that could be the subject of an entire book. One way to do that is to ask the customer about twenty questions, at least, to find out what his wants are as well as his needs. Then some good thought (this is where real creativity, some people say intelligence, along with perseverance and empathy, come in) should be given before attempting to convince the customer that for his own good his wants should be modified to fit the needs or the needs should be modified to fit the wants. Possibly both could be modified to meet in the middle. Without such a dialogue, any move forward is a risky one and usually a temporary one.

Testing Wants And Needs

How to test is a logical and often asked question. One way of course is to look for consistency in answers. If the answers are not consistent one must go back over them again to find out whether they are not consistent due to insincerity or confusion or possibly just a change of mind. It is important to know which it is and then to try to determine what is the "real McCoy." What are the real needs and wants? This is admittedly easier said than done. However, it is amazing to me how simple and effortless a professional salesperson makes it appear. Another way to test, of course, is the old reliable way of supplying a sample or a prototype of the product or service to see how it is evaluated by the customer. Then, after the prototype or sample has been delivered and inspected by the customer, more questions are often needed to come even closer to determining what the real needs and wants are.

So what does this have to do with relationships? The answer to this is really quite simple. Just ask yourself, how do you feel about the company that really knows what you need and want and "understands" you as opposed to the one who constantly tries to sell to you something that you don't need or don't really want? Whom would you rather do business with? Whom would you rather talk to? Or to put it in personal terms, if you have one friend who seems to "understand" how you feel about things and you have another friend who doesn't, whom do you trust? Whom would you rather spend time with? Whom can you depend on?

THE BALDOR VALUE FORMULA

$$V_p = \frac{Q_p \times S_p}{C \times T}$$

This formula, sometimes called an equation even though it is not a mathematical equation, has been successfully used by us at Baldor for almost twenty years. It has been successful for us in planning and training, but it has also been very beneficial in real-life situations, even very stressful ones.

V_p is based on the assumption, and we think a good one, that value is what customers instinctively look for. Whether they are analytical or go by the seat of their pants, value is what they want and what they will compare. Here again the customer's perception of the value of relationships, as his perception of the value of the product, is what really counts. Therefore, companies who offer good value, and this is perceived by the customer as good value, will prosper. Those who do not do both of these will fade away.

Here is what we mean by each of the four independent variables:

1. Q_p is not quality as we measure it (and we have many measures of it). It is what the *customers* perceive. This is more difficult to measure, but it is definitely more relevant.

2. S_p is service. Here again as perceived by the customer. This goes beyond the usual meaning of the word service and includes what the customer thinks of the company, the distributor or dealer, the salespeople, the company's reputation, the distributor's and salespeople's reputations. Possibly most important of all is the perception of the customer of whether or not the company will stand behind the product. Also, there is a whole new area that is becoming more important as a part of perceived service and that is information—its availability and accuracy. While we realize that information is not included in most textbooks under service, we do so here. This, we find, is where the customers include this important variable.

3. C, of course, stands for cost. This could also be defined as price, but since we are looking at it from the customer's point of view, the supplier's price is seen to the customer as cost. Also, cost often includes add-ons to the price such as freight and other charges.

4. T is time. Being a denominator, the lower the amount of time, the higher the value. Time here generally means the number of minutes, hours, days, or weeks between the time a product or service is requested or ordered and the time it is delivered or received. All of us in business are now more and more acutely aware that one of our goals is to reduce this time if we are to remain competitive.

As the formula or equation says, equal weight is given to these four independent variables. All situations are different. Even though one can easily think of a situation in which one of these elements is most important, experience has shown us that in the long run, each of the four have about equal importance. This has been tested many times and, whereas in an emergency, T is dominant or where, as one of our students once said, when you are sitting on top of a rocket being shot into outer space, Q is most important, in the long run and in most cases all four are important. Making one predominant over the others is a distortion of the true situation. We realize that many textbooks have zeroed in on Q, and while we realize it is a very important variable, we contend, and our tests have shown, that the other three are equally as important.

Further, definitions are a problem here. Quality means different things to different people. To some it means measurable according to a company's own formula (often at odds with what a customer might perceive). To others it means performance. To others it means durability or reliability. To some, consistency, or all of the above.

To sum up, we believe in the formula and we believe this formula illustrates what happens in real life—that we actually buy value. One opportunity to check this out is the next time you make a major purchase—a car, a pickup, a house, a major appliance. Examine, after you have made the purchase, how you arrived at your purchase decision. Was is the lowest price that earned your vote? Was it the highest quality? Or was it a combination of the two plus availability, throwing in an important consideration of the reputation of the seller? Or as many people say when they test themselves, "All of the above."

One thing is for sure, the supplier or vendor who understands what the customers want and what they are thinking, has a great competitive advantage over the supplier who doesn't have this understanding. This formula is an attempt to organize this type of thinking and understanding.

Testing With Chips

Another way to test and to learn a customers needs and wants is with a method we have used at Baldor for a number of years. We made four little plastic chips of four different colors, each representing one of the four independent variables in the Value Formula: Quality, Service, Cost, and Time. We then present these one at a time to the customer and ask questions about each one as it relates to the customer.

Quality is the most logical one to start with. By putting down the little chip representing Quality, it makes it easier to ask questions about the customer's definition of quality. Does he think it is more a matter of durability, or consistency, or performance of the product? Or is it perceived in the lack of maintenance, ease of use—or what is it—in his mind? Certainly this can be done without a "prop", but we have found that the little chips certainly help.

Then we found that the next logical one to use is the Cost chip. The normal response here is that the customer says, "Naturally cost is important. That is what I have been telling you." Then some questions could logically follow up to attempt to find out what the customer means by "being competitive." And also what he includes in cost, such as extras. For example, is the freight included in the cost? Are there extra charges included in his definition of cost or is that price only?

After Quality and Cost, Time is the logical one to use next. To most customers this means availability. How important is this to the customer? To some customers, and in some circumstances, this could be, and often is, the most important variable of all. Occasionally, but less and less frequently—you can find this out by asking—it is not a very important factor. It is important to know how vital it is. Often the seller/provider/vendor can adjust or adapt to the customer's requirements for time and availability. Unless the supplier knows quite accurately, however, what the customer expects, it is difficult for him to adapt to meet this expectation.

Just in Time (JIT) has become more popular as a management concept.

Whether we agree with these concepts or not, the fact is that many customers do—some fervently. The importance of time is increasing.

Then the real "clincher" is the chip that says Service. This is usually followed by a question from the customer, "What do you mean by service?" I believe if you will look at *Webster*'s you will find anywhere from 20 to 30 definitions (depending upon the version or size) for the word. It can mean anything from what you get (good or bad) in a restaurant, to what a bull does for a cow, to the initial point of a tennis match, or to what you attend on Sunday mornings at church. What we mean here is a mixture of many things, all the way from the reputation of the company (in the customer's mind, of course) to the customer's perception as to whether the company will stand behind the product, availability of parts, quality and timeliness of any repairs that may be needed, right down to whether the customer trusts the seller or not. Also, we have been finding during the last few years that, more and more, the very important subject of information (quality and availability) is included in the customer's definition of service. We realize that many put information in a different category, but with many dozens of tests with customers we are finding they are considering it part of service.

For example, just the other day, we had a very good customer tell us, "I get really good service when I call your Los Angeles office. They almost always have the information I need and they give it to me quickly." He wasn't talking about repairs or parts; he was talking about the availability and quality of information.

Then, if time permits, we push these four little chips at random around the table and ask the customer to rank them in order of importance to him—not what the book says, not what somebody else says, but to him or her in his or her opinion. In other words, "Would you be so kind, Mr. Customer, as to rank these in order of importance to you when you make an important buying decision?"

Our testing and experience shows that most customers, particularly the most aggressive ones—the most important ones—will do this. They'll work at it. The only ones who won't play the game are the ones who aren't too important to you anyway. These are bureaucratic-minded types who don't want to express an opinion at all. Most entrepreneurs and experienced managers will spend quite a bit of time, anywhere from two or three up to as long as ten minutes, arranging these four chips in order of importance. They will usually start out putting Cost (price) at the top, then Quality, and then Time (availability), with Service at the bottom. Then the more they think about it they will say, "Service is mighty important; I don't want to buy from somebody I don't trust," or "I don't want to buy from people who won't stand behind their product," so Service starts moving its way up.

Then availability or Time moves its way up with such remarks as, "What is the use of getting the best quality or even the lowest price if I can't get the product (or service) when I need it?" The net result is usually that they line all four up as equals. This, of course, is exactly what the Baldor Value Formula says. You will notice that the formula does not put a weight on any one of the four independent variables. Therefore it gives them equal importance. Once in a while, someone, usually a very experienced person, will put Service at the top with Quality and Time and Cost as equals but below Service. But usually, all four are ranked as equals or approximate equals.

This exercise with the four chips has proven invaluable to us in learning about our customers and in building stronger relationships with them. They give the seller the opportunity to double, triple, or even quadruple his knowledge of what the customer really thinks is important, what he really needs (left-brain thinking) and also the way he feels about things (right-brain thinking).

Customer Relationships On The Information Highway

Much has been written and said in the last few years about the "information highway". There have been some tremendous improvements in communication. The fax machine has really been a miracle. We have computers able to store huge amounts of information, collate them and retrieve them on command. We also have pagers, cellular telephones, and the Internet.

These are all wonderful tools. But as good carpenter tools need good carpenters to handle them, so it is with the information tools with which we now have to work. No doubt about it, there is still no substitute for face-to-face contact with customers; namely, people sitting down and talking to people—people building good relationships.

The new idea that personal contact with customers can be eliminated by having computers talking to computers is simply impractical. It has been tried by many, but only in special situations does the idea really work.

The good news, however, is that in the hands of well-trained and effective salespeople, these new information tools greatly improve productivity. A skilled and experienced salesperson today can probably produce two or even three times the results possible ten or fifteen years ago. Face to face with a customer, when tough questions came up a few years ago, the common answer usually was, "I'll get the information and get back to you tomorrow (or next week or next month)." Now with laptops and modems and instant communication the answer can usually be secured in a matter of minutes. This greatly improves relationships with customers and, also, greatly increases the productivity of the salesperson. When well-trained and well-motivated salespeople are paired up with the new "tools", the results are wonderful.

Relationships are strengthened for the simple reason that the salesperson is able to give the customer the information he wants more quickly and more completely. Then after the customer has the information he needs, the next step is to secure the order. This in turn is entered with the company much more quickly. It is therefore delivered more quickly, completely, and accurately to the customer. Customers love this quick service. They go to companies that provide it. As time goes by, the successful customer—supplier relationship becomes stronger and stronger. It becomes very difficult for a competitor to break in.

That is, unless the supplier becomes self-satisfied or overconfident or, even worse, arrogant. This often is called the "price of success" but could more accurately be called the "price of stupidity." This deterioration of a relationship, when either party becomes arrogant, almost always ends up with the relationship becoming weaker and, ultimately, broken.

Lost Customers

The American Society for Quality Control once ran a rather extensive study showing reasons why companies lose customers. Of course, as you would imagine, they thought that lack of quality of the product would be a very large factor.

What they found was different. They found that only 14 percent of customer loss was due to dissatisfaction with the product itself. A much larger number, 68 percent, were turned away by an attitude of indifference by a company employee. Isn't that quite similar to saying that they were not treated by the supplier as being important? Or could it also be said that the relationship became weak due to lack of attention or indifference or neglect? They came to the conclusion, which surprised them, that good customer service was such an important factor that they concluded by saying, "Unless the customer is completely satisfied—to the point of being positively delighted and willing to brag about the product or service received—there exists great potential for market damage and further trouble for the company (seller)." Well said!

The most common way of damaging or destroying a good relationship is to take it for granted. Or, even worse, to ignore it. Being ignored, to many, is even worse than being insulted or reviled.

Even if there are 5,000 customers involved and only a few leave, it is vitally important for the supplier to find out why. Without knowing why, the manufacturer/supplier is "shooting craps", or betting that the loss is some irrelevant event or the result of an "unreasonable" customer or a "one of a kind" odd event. If the supplier gambles this way and is right, no harm is done. If he is wrong and it becomes a trend, great harm can and probably will be done.

One of the best and most effective television ads ever was the one run several years ago by United Airlines. In it the boss had called all 20 or 30 of his key people together for what appeared to be a rather grim meeting. He started out by announcing that their best customer had just "fired them." He said the reason was that they had phoned them and faxed them and called them again and faxed them again, but nobody had been to see them.

He then announced that they were going to call on every customer face to face to rebuild relationships. When one of the staff members pointed out that it meant going to 40 or 50 cities, he said, "Yes." He then started handing out United Airlines tickets. When asked what he was going to do, as he walked away with his ticket sticking out of his back pocket, he said, "I am going to see the customer that fired us today."

No doubt about it, face-to-face contact with customers is absolutely vital to building good relationships with them. That's what's so great about this message conveyed in this amazingly lucid one-minute commercial. Isn't it amazing how in one minute a good commercial can tell a whole story?

What Makes A Good Customer

Although it is a risky practice, there is much value in attempting to evaluate customers. What constitutes a good customer? Amateurs go by size, but there are several other considerations. There are some guidelines that have been used successfully and practically for many years. One set of guidelines states that a good customer has the following six characteristics:

1. Sales Volume. This first factor is easily measured. While an important one, it is far from the only one.

2. Profitability. Most studies show wide variation in profitability from one customer to another, one type to another, one area to another.

3. Repeatability. Particularly to manufacturers (and wholesalers and retailers as well), customers who buy with some sort of regularity and predictability are much easier to handle. Therefore, they are more desirable than those who are unpredictable and spasmodic.

4. Financial Strength/Creditworthiness. Whether the customer is large or small, financial status and ability to pay on time or approximately on time is always an important factor. When the seller is undercapitalized, this factor rises to the top as being one of the very most important factors of all.

5. Adaptability/Suitability. Some customers fit the capabilities of the supplier to a "T". This, of course, makes them desirable. Relationships tend to be good when there is that fit. Aggressive people probably

should, and do, stretch in the interest of securing more business, growth and expansion. However, the more the customer's wants and needs differ from the capabilities of their suppliers, the more difficult it is to establish good relationships.

6. Reputation/Standing in the Community/Well Thought of in the Industry. Customers who are leaders help attract more customers.

Myths And Misconceptions Affecting Customer Relationships
Baldor Electric and I, personally, are often referred to as contrarians. One of our recent annual reports had as its theme, "The Road Less Traveled," in which we pointed out a number of important decisions the company had made that at the time seemed contrary to general business practices. Some of these included manufacturing in the USA when many in our industry were moving abroad, carrying large inventories when the style was the opposite, and doing everything possible to avoid layoffs in tough times.

One reason for our going down this "road less traveled" was that we feel that some businesses make decisions based on business myths or misconceptions. Some of these widespread myths or misconceptions give guidance on how to take care of customers and build stronger customer relationships.

MYTH I: Inventories are evil.
One of the most common misconceptions we see coming out of business schools is the disaffection, or even hostility, toward manufacturers carrying finished goods inventories. While this is particularly true in the case of manufacturers this is also true among retailers and

wholesalers. In other words, the myth is, "The less inventory, the better." This begs the question, "Better for whom?" Certainly not better for the customers. Nor is it better for the employees, but we will get to this in a later chapter.

Some investigation shows what is behind this myth is that many calculations are made on the costs of carrying inventories. Often these are called carrying costs. There are lots of different formulas and, rather than arguing whether more inventory should be carried or less, most of the academic arguments have to do with the proper method of measuring inventory costs.

Many people struggle with why their instincts tell them they should carry more inventories while their financial people and "brains" tell them to carry less. The main reason is really quite simple. It is the fact that the costs of carrying inventories are measurable and calculable while the costs of *not* carrying inventories are difficult to measure. Therefore, if one follows the old chestnut of "If you can't count it, it doesn't count," the carrying costs win out every time, and inventories are cut to the bone.

We have no quarrel with any of these measures of carrying costs, but we do vehemently disagree, as do many other experienced manufacturers, wholesalers and retailers, with the entire concept. What about the costs of *not* having good inventories? Is this calculated? Is it calculable? If estimates are acceptable, and they certainly are in many other accounting and reporting endeavors, why not here? Shouldn't this be based on an estimate of lost sales due to lack of inventory plus possible or even probable loss of productivity?

Maybe even most important of all, loss of customers?

Incidentally, this is an area where accountants really shudder when you ask them to calculate the cost of losing a customer. Idea: There have been many calculations of the costs of securing a new customer. Then wouldn't it be logical to say that the cost of losing a similar one is about the same?

Another way to look at this is to contend that the people making the decision to cut down inventories are making three assumptions. Not only are these assumptions not true, but the assumers often don't even see they are making these assumptions.

> A. The first assumption is that the carrying costs are higher than the profits derived from extra sales by providing better service to customers. As mentioned, the sales that are lost by cutting down service levels to customers are not easily measurable. Even the best measurements are full of estimates and more assumptions. Therefore, they are usually not made at all. On top of the costs of the loss of sales are many other costs due to lack of inventory that are also difficult to measure. These have to do with extra sales expense incurred by not having inventories, namely more rush orders, more air freight or delivery charges, higher communications costs, and most important to manufacturers, the extra costs of running rush orders through production. Special orders are also costly to retailers and wholesalers.

> B. A second assumption is made that the level of finished

goods inventory has nothing to do with production or service costs. In manufacturing this is a very large factor, namely, the lower cost of running stock orders compared to rush special orders.

C. A third assumption is that there is no impact on competitive advantage. What is a competitive advantage worth? Who knows? Everyone knows that a competitive advantage is very valuable, but here again it is not measurable. Therefore, the competitive advantage of maintaining good customer service by having better inventories and "full shelves" as opposed to the opposite (which most experienced people know is a very large factor) is not usually put into the model or taken into account or considered in the paradigm. It should be, as it's big. Michael Porter, professor of business at Harvard, wrote, "Competitive advantage is at the heart of a firm's performance."

MYTH II:

Small customers are costly/profit losers — get rid of them.

There have been several recent examples of companies acting on this myth. One that received a lot of publicity recently was the announcement by Levi-Strauss that any of their customers that hadn't bought at least $9,000 worth of merchandise by a certain amount of time would no longer be able to buy direct from the company. This was received with a storm of protest, often by old-time customers. Many claimed that they had put the company "on the map."

Three important assumptions are apparently made by those who want to get rid of small customers. While these assumptions were definitely made, they are in most cases not stated or included in models or calculations.

A. Small customers stay small. This has been disproved many times. One study that we participated in had to do with the history of our company's 50 largest customers. Using a definition of small as any customer buying less than $100,000 of product per year for several years, the study showed the amazing number of 42 of these 50 large customers were once small customers for several years. What if they had been neglected, or even worse, cut off, when they were small? How then would they have ever become large customers? Once the seller found the value years later of these small customers that grew up, what would be the chances of forming a good relationship after years of neglect or rejection?

B. Small orders come from small customers. Granted, small orders can often be a pain in the neck to retailers, wholesalers, and particularly to manufacturers. All good operating people look for any way possible to avoid small orders and there are several ways to do this. (One of the most successful is with a modification capability.) Here again the assumption is simply not true. Several studies have shown that some of the largest quantities of small orders come from large customers. Many manufacturers report that some of their largest customers bombard them with small orders on almost a daily basis; many of these requiring special setups, special schedules, special delivery, etc. Now whether small orders should be eliminated or lessened in one way or another is another point. The point here is that the assumption that they come from small customers is wrong.

C. Profit margins are the same or even worse with small customers than with large customers. No way! Most manufacturers and wholesalers sell to small customers at what is usually known as book price or standard price. Meanwhile, while many don't want to elaborate on this or even admit it, large customers demand, and often receive, special and sometimes expensive service and large discounts that small customers don't get. Most models showing the "evils" of small customers do not take this into account.

In addition to the fact that these three assumptions are usually made (but not even realized) in the increasingly popular practice of getting rid of the little guys (or giving them a reduced level of service), there are other factors which mitigate against tossing out the little guy. In many cases, as in the Levi-Strauss example, many of the company's oldest and most loyal customers are indeed small. They are the ones that require very little attention, seldom complain, and rarely demand extra service. In many respects they are the model customers, except for the one factor of low volume.

We have many small customers. We consider them to be the heart of our business. It is difficult to prove, but many of our experienced people feel this way. One small customer, out of many, comes to mind who has been extremely helpful from an "idea" point of view. He is outspoken, in a friendly way, he is very supportive, and most important to us, he is very aware of what is going on in his field. He is better than any consultant we could hire in his field. In addition, he has referred other customers to us, some of whom are small and others who are middle-sized or large. What if we had gotten rid of him?

MYTH III:

Throwing more money at a problem will help solve it.

Amazingly enough, some of the same people who work very hard to control expenses, even to the detriment of the company, will occasionally "throw money at a problem." This is often done emotionally.

It is becoming more and more apparent that this is more a problem of the "old school". In all fairness, some recent MBAs seem to have a better understanding of people and what motivates employees. We are finding this to be increasingly true of those who call themselves "night MBAs". We find that many MBAs quite proudly differentiate themselves from "day MBAs" as being those who have been out in the world, who have had business experience, and then returned to earn their MBAs.

The reason why otherwise logical management people pursue such an illogical approach is based on the "pet product" or "pet project" syndrome. This is an easy trap to fall into, particularly for aggressive people. Managers are people also. They have emotions and prejudices which often work against them. Rather than abandoning an unsuccessful project, they will often pursue it with even more vigor and money.

MYTH IV:

We can save our way to prosperity.

There is a paradoxical practice spreading throughout industry during the last few years that says, "We can save our way to prosperity" by cutting expenses. In a "no growth" company, there may be few alternatives, but why even accept the "no growth" concept?

Numbers-oriented people often go to their bosses with plans to "save x dollars." Sometimes these projects are very worthwhile, but sometimes they are not. The most common type of cost saving project that is not the way to go is when the savings are made at the cost of customer relationships. The originators of the project often "prove" there will be a certain amount of savings per month or year.

Here again an assumption is often made and not stated. This assumption is that this sort of savings, made at the expense of customer service, will have no effect on revenue or top line. Of course, any detrimental effect on top line will have a detrimental effect on bottom line, and very often more than the cost savings.

We saw an amusing and rather small example of this in our headquarters' town. Our directors visit here four or five times a year. They had a favorite place to stay. It is not the largest or even the most prestigious, but the directors liked the service they received. One of the favorite services was that this establishment supplied a pot of hot coffee and a newspaper shortly after the wake-up call.

One morning having breakfast with the directors, I found them to be in a gloomy mood. When I asked them why, hoping it had no relation to anything the company had done, I found that they hadn't received their coffee and newspaper that morning. One of the directors had inquired at the desk about this, and after working his way up to the assistant manager, was told that, "We have discontinued this." When asked why, he said, "We have saved $17,000 per year by cutting out the coffee and newspapers." Our director told him that they could "just keep" their $17,000 savings, but that this was one of the reasons they had been staying here. The directors then decided they would just go to the larger and more prestigious hotel in the future.

Fortunately, reason prevailed. Upon hearing this, the hotel reestablished their previous service. But if they had stuck to their plan, would they have really saved $17,000? Or would they have lost $20,000, or more?

MYTH V:.

Cutting out slow-moving products can save a lot of money without doing any damage to other products or projects.

This myth is a really dangerous one because it sounds so logical. It sounds sensible because slow-moving products are a "drag," particularly to manufacturing people.

Most manufacturing people worth their salt continually point out the need to improve productivity by cutting out small orders and slow-moving products. They quite logically show that keeping the old tooling or the old inventories necessary to support these products is not only expensive but it slows down production of "winning products" and/or "winning services." While it is often the right thing to do, it is sometimes the wrong thing to do. Those that do not approach this problem with a little bit of caution and thought are the ones that believe you can reach into a jar full of 500 marbles and pull one out without any of the other 499 moving.

I think in college business schools this has been called "product rationalization." Models are made. It appears as if it is almost always the right thing to do. It certainly is if the gain is greater than the loss. But what about the loss? Isn't there an implied assumption by many that the loss is zero, because it is not even estimated or put into the model or the equation? If someone objects to calling it a zero, just ask, "Where is it? Don't see it?"

Then the common objection is, "How are you going to measure it?" This appears to get back to the old saw, "If you can't count it, it doesn't count." The answer, of course, is that you estimate it, same as many other factors in planning and accounting.

This brings up the question of how do you estimate it. The top-line loss would be the revenue lost from associated products and the bottom-line loss would be the profits on the surviving products not sold, because of the change. Also, if product rationalization is carried to the extreme, and it sometimes is, the remaining products would usually go up in cost, rather than down, for the obvious reason that they must share more of the overhead. Unless the overhead is cut by an equal or greater amount than the loss of revenue, naturally the cost of the remaining products will go up (unless productivity catches up rapidly with the loss).

Therefore, to sum up, this is another example of, "There is no substitute for judgement." Is cutting products always a good thing to do? Experience shows us that sometimes it is and sometimes it isn't.

Crises In Customer Relationships

Building strong relationships has many benefits for both sides. In addition to the obvious benefits of better results, better productivity, being on a "winning team", etc. there is the not so obvious benefit of having more fun. Fun is a word that didn't even appear in business books till the last few years. It is still scorned by some purists.

But what about relationships during crisis situations? Strong relationships resist breakage during periods of storm and strife. There are several types of crises or serious events which can damage or destroy relationships. These range all the way from quality problems, to poor service, to price problems, to lack of availability, and to technological change.

One of the best old-time professional salesmen I ever knew had a theory that went something like: "Until you've had some real trouble with a customer, you don't know them and they don't really know you." When I first heard this theory of his I rather argumentatively asked him if he actually "welcomed" trouble. "No," he said, "but I know an opportunity when I see one." He gave several examples of customers who were buying from several suppliers, including him. When trouble did occur, he saw to it that his company outperformed his competitors. He made sure the bosses knew about it, and he came out of the stress and strife in a much stronger position than he went in. In other words, he established strong relationships with his customers which often his competitors did not.

Trouble in a relationship may provide a serendipitous opportunity for success. One of the most serendipitous events in our company's history occurred many years ago when we were small and poor. Our largest customer was very unhappy with us. We had some quality problems on our part which were very distressing to this customer and needed immediate correction. The customer was located 500 miles away and it would have been very expensive for us to have called in a local shop to make necessary reconnections and repairs. Therefore, we decided it would be less expensive to send two of our assemblers right off the factory floor.

The results were amazing! Not only did these two assemblers get the job done—they proved to be very competent in solving problems—but much to our surprise (I've seen it many times since), they did marvelous work in reestablishing good relationships with the customer.

They found there was much work to do with five or six hundred heavy motors. It would have taken two people several weeks to do the job alone. Therefore, they did a good "Tom Sawyer" job. By working hard the first day or two, they gradually accumulated some allies and helpers. The next step was they got better acquainted. Then they showed the customer, including not only the bosses but the people on their factory floor, what well-built motors these actually were. Then, when they were properly connected and tested, they showed what a superior product we were manufacturing.

Later I talked to the boss, our customer. He was a very angry man before our two assemblers appeared on the scene. He was very close to getting another supplier. After they got the job done, he was one of the biggest boosters of our company and has been ever since.

What really happened there? Our two good guys off the factory floor got together with their good guys on their factory floor, found that they had a lot in common, found they could help each other out, found that they were important to each other, and then proceeded to get the job done. Then, after they got the job done, there was a feeling of comradeship built up very similar to that of an athletic team after it has won a key game. Then the next step was that we bosses saw the good effects on both companies, and our relationship improved. The improvement was drastic, not just incremental.

Then there is the "unusual event." This by definition may happen only once a decade or maybe even less frequently than that. This type of emergency or crisis may be caused by a large technological change. The old classical story here is the manufacturer of the best buggy whips in town who is giving good service to his customers in a rapidly shrinking market. Or, in modern times, the excellent radio vacuum tube manufacturer being rapidly replaced by solid-state electronics 30 years ago.

What does this have to do with relationships? Simple. If relationships are strong between the supplier and the customer, the customer will be tipping off the manufacturer far ahead of time that this crisis is coming, The customer with a strong relationship with his supplier wants this relationship to continue. It is well agreed that when any of us have good relationships we want these relationships to continue and strengthen. Therefore, in good relationships, the manufacturer/supplier is not caught by surprise. Not only is he tipped off by customers and salespeople that this change is coming, but with the good relationship he is often given good coaching as to what direction to move in to be able to weather this technological storm.

Some vacuum tube manufacturers disappeared, some switched to solid-state slowly and limped along, others welcomed the new technology and mightily prospered.

Another type of customer crisis occurs when there is a breakthrough in manufacturing techniques that allows a product to be produced at a much lower cost or much more quickly. When this happens the manufacturer who has not yet embraced this technology is in trouble. Good relationships here help in two ways. First, in the way described above, by getting advanced warning from the customers, and second, customers who feel "good" about their suppliers will be more patient, will give the supplier more time to recover, before "fleeing the coop."

An example of technological change that helped an excellent company change from a product loser to a winner was Hewlett-Packard's handling of their line of printers. A few years ago this was considered the weak area of their computer line. Many of their customers, including us, complained about the old ink-jet printer. It had many shortcomings. In other words, we customers did not feel it did as good a job as other H-P equipment. It didn't turn out the quality it should. H-P listened to the customers, made a major effort, and leapfrogged the competitors. They came out with a printer that was the top of the line. Within a relatively short time they had the lion's share of the market. This helped greatly in selling allied products. Without good relationships with both their customers and employees, would or could this have happened?

Boundarylessness

The interesting concept of boundarylessness, expounded frequently by Jack Welch, CEO of General Electric, has a strong effect on a company's ability to give improved customer service. The whole idea of boundarylessness is not a new concept, although it is discussed more today than previously. In past years it was known as "knocking the walls down" or "improving teamwork between departments."

Boundarylessness as it refers to customer relationships makes a lot of sense. It allows a company to marshall more resources—and more quickly—to respond to customers' needs.

There are many natural, human-nature type resistances to boundarylessness. One of the strongest, in engineering, is known as the "not invented here" syndrome. In finance it is, "If you don't have a degree in finance or an MBA, what do you know about money and capital?" Marketing people continually complain that everyone thinks he or she is a marketing expert.

We have had many good and successful examples of boundarylessness helping us with problems, allowing us to do things for customers that we otherwise could not have done. We had an example recently where a good customer needed some special software for electronic drives that he wanted to buy from us. In our entire engineering group we only had a few people who were capable of producing this software, and they were up to their ears in other projects. Therefore, the needs of this very good customer were being postponed to the detriment of this customer and our relationship.

In a face-to-face discussion with the customer one day, where we were trying to explain the reasons for the delays, it struck us (right in the middle of this conversation) that we were not thinking in a boundarylessness way. Thinking in the conventional way, we had in that design engineering group only two or three people who were capable of doing this work. Actually we had six, seven, or eight other people capable of developing this software, but they were in the Information Services Department, were not design engineers, and were, therefore, not even considered.

Upon trying this idea out on some of our people, we ran immediately into two negative reactions. The first one had to do with the difference in computer language while the other was something along the lines of, "They wouldn't be interested or wouldn't want to tackle this project. It isn't in their field."

The answer to the first one was that indeed the Information Services Department worked with many languages, including the engineering language. A positive answer to the second negative response was that we would just ask for volunteers and see what happened. We did this and immediately four or five volunteers appeared, all of whom were experienced software designers and programmers. They were eager to participate in this program. The result was a tripling or quadrupling of the available resources to do what our good customer wanted us to do. Thinking conventionally, this could not have been done.

Conclusion

To sum up, as Peter Drucker says, customers are the reason for a business (or hospital or university) to be in existence. Therefore, it would be tempting—even possibly correct—to refer to them as the most important constituency. To do this, however, would be to deny this importance balance—balance between the three constituencies—good relationships with customers, employees and owners (shareholders). So let's turn to the next vitally important constituency: employees.

EMPLOYEES

Introduction

Good relationships with employees are absolutely vital for success in any venture, large or small, profit or nonprofit. There is no way to take good care of customers, and shareholders as well, without good employees. Good employees are those who are capable and want to do a good job for the company and its customers. And if they do a good job for the company and its customers, shareholders will also benefit.

Companies often don't know what employees want; although in recent years, some recognition is being developed. This is partly thanks to some great consultants and authors. One is Charles Hughes who writes about ways to improve relationships with employees. He says, "Improving communications which isn't really costly," and that "The open door is cheap and the job posting system is inexpensive." Also he suggests, "Training and education doesn't cost much." But he says that without doing these good things, we would be right back where we were a generation ago, namely, with a company or the management of the company not really knowing what is important to the employees.

Where would we be in marketing if we didn't know what our customers want and need? We would be in bad shape. That is where we would be. I think most people would agree with that. Why then don't people agree that we would be in equally bad condition if we didn't know what our employees want and need? Why do some companies spend millions of dollars (properly, usually) surveying and questioning customers without doing the same thing in their own offices and shops with their own employees?

The Wall Street Journal reported recently on the Roger Stark Worldwide, Inc., "A Dream In Danger" study showing that of 2000 workers surveyed, worker contentment was at its lowest point in the last 20 years. They were referring to satisfaction with hours, opportunities, benefits, comradeship, and work's contribution to society. Twenty years ago this survey showed 4 out of 10 workers deemed themselves "extremely satisfied," where, in using the same criteria, the number now is only 1 in 4.

Assuming this is true, and several other studies have shown similar results, why isn't more attention being paid to employee relationships? Sure, good companies do it, but how many good companies are there? Why do some companies have only 6 percent employee turnover a year, some 16 percent, and some even as high as 60-70 percent? In fact, there are some industries with high turnover where managers seem to worry less than those with little turnover.

Okay, there is a problem. Now what can be done to improve employee relationships? What elements are needed to secure and keep good employees and ensure good long-term relationships with them? Here are some of the most important.

Meaningful Work

"Sense of mission" has been written about by many. Usually this is management's, a consultant's, or a professor's sense of mission. Let's look at this from an employee's point of view. What is meaningful from the employee's perspective?

To many people, manufacturing a useful product is very meaningful. To others, talking to and taking care of customers is satisfying, sometimes stimulating. Different people have widely different concepts of what is meaningful. This is fortunate. Otherwise, everyone would want to do the same job and leave others undone.

Further, what is meaningful to a person at one age may not be at another. When one considers differences in interests, education, native abilities, aggressiveness, age and many other factors, one could wonder how anyone ever gets to the right job at the right place. Not easy. But the challenge to both employees and employers is to find the right spot for the right person.

Employees often can find the right place for themselves if given the opportunity. Open bidding in manufacturing and the ability to change jobs in service companies was, and often still is, frowned upon. The reason usually given was a simple and apparently logical one, but it often ended with bad results.

The reason given for lack of employee mobility was often called "loss of skills." There are lots of old expressions that go something like, "Don't try to turn a piano player into a place kicker" or other such seemingly logical but incorrect points of view. Therefore, a welder usually remained a welder the rest of his life, a machinist remained a machinist, and so on. But providing employees the opportunity to find the right place for themselves can often have very positive results for the employee and the employer.

In terms of job placement and/or mobility, does a company succeed by doing what is best for the company or best for the employee? Possibly in the short term a company will do better by keeping the welder as a welder. But it is becoming more and more apparent that, in the long run, giving the employee the opportunity to do what is meaningful to him will be best for both.

Another way of saying this is that, if possible, the employee should be given a chance to do what he feels good about doing in helping to fulfill the mission of the company. This is one of the many reasons that everyone in the company should know what the company's mission is and be able to put it in their own terms.

A couple of old-time employees once told me that the test, from their point of view, as to whether their work was meaningful, was whether they welcomed this question from their small child, "What do you do at work, Daddy?" Not only whether they could answer the question, but whether they were proud and pleased to do so was the test.

Several years ago at an open house at Baldor, I happened to notice a young lad about ten years old wandering through the closed machine shop. He was alone, and I was wondering if he was lost. Upon striking up a conversation with him, I found that he was not at all lost.

He was admiring some of our new CNC (computer numerically controlled) lathes and chuckers.

He was a bright lad, quite conversational, eager to talk. After asking a few questions, like where he lived and where he went to school, I ventured to ask him what he wanted to do when he grew up. He had a prompt answer. He said, "When I grow up I want to work on a CNC at Baldor like my daddy does." Does that young man's father feel that his work is meaningful? You bet!

There's an old story about three stonecutters working diligently at their trade. Upon inquiry as to what they were doing, the first one said he was chipping the stones as required and instructed by his boss. The second one appeared to be a little more interested than the first and more conversant as well. He said he was proud to do a good job of cutting the stone so that they would have straight and square sides, thereby allowing them to fit together well.

The third stonecutter was working hard. He not only appeared to be enjoying what he was doing, but also had an air about him that said he was doing something important. When asked what he was doing he simply said he was "Building a cathedral." Now there was a man who was doing meaningful work!

Back in the summer of 1988, during the hot election campaign between Vice President George Bush and Governor Michael Dukakis, our governor at that time, Bill Clinton, was actively campaigning for Dukakis and for his own reelection as governor. During that time, he came to talk to our employees here in Fort Smith. In fact, this was the day after he had appeared on the Johnny Carson program where the main theme was Johnny ribbing him about his overly-long nomination speech at the Democratic Convention.

Despite very little sleep the previous night and the media's ragging him about his long speech, he made an excellent talk to our employees. The main subject of his talk was to tell everyone here that what they were doing was important. He said it in a very straightforward and credible way.

> "When you see those individual workers putting together those motors like I saw today, in times that I found unbelievable when I asked how long it took, you are striking a blow not just to keep your jobs and increase your incomes but also to insure the future of this company. You cannot possibly imagine how important this is. The economic and political security of this country rests as much on the backs of the American manufacturing community as it does with our ships in the Persian Gulf, with our radar warning systems in North Dakota, and with our troops in Europe, because we cannot maintain any of that without a strong economy, so we have a lot riding on your success here."

The response from our employees, as you would surmise, was excellent. Many of them said to me later that what the governor said confirmed to them what they had thought all along; that what they are doing is important. They think it is important to a lot of people, including our customers and shareholders; important also to the strength of our country and the strength of our economy. What they do is indeed meaningful.

Recognition

Recognition can take the form of plaques, profit sharing (extremely important in terms of recognition and free enterprise, itself), pins, and a multitude of other tangible objects. I have been surprised to find that a mention in the company newsletter by name, particularly tied to some achievement, is a very important type of recognition. Then there are subjective forms such as the sense of belonging to a good organization, recognition by peers and superiors of the employees' contribution to the company, achieving the company's mission, and personal relationships among coworkers. Also a sense of participation in the progress and growth and excellence of the company is an important feeling even beyond the sense of belonging.

This feeling of being important in the growth and excellence of the company can be fostered among employees when they are encouraged to develop relationships with customers. In the "old-fashioned" or "cold" company, say for example with a thousand employees, there were probably only 10 people in the whole company who really knew the customers or had much contact with them. The modern company and the successful company with 1,000 employees probably has at least a 100 or sometimes more, maybe a ratio of 10 to 1, over the old-fashioned cold company of those who have relationships with customers.

To many people, a simple "good morning" or a nod of the head is an important form of recognition. Many times, as Dale Carnegie so well brings out in his great books, simply calling a person by name is important. Or as he points out so often, sincere flattery (he emphasizes it must be sincere and earned) is a wonderful form of recognition.

One of the real experts in recognizing employees, as he was in many other things, was Sam Walton of Wal-Mart. Sam referred to all the employees as "associates," and he really meant it. From personal observation during several opportunities I had to travel with Sam to his stores, I noted that he spent most of his time building relationships with employees. When he had only a few hundred employees, he could call them all by name. As the company grew larger, to make sure that he could continue to call employees by name, he had everybody, including himself, wear name tags. The name tags had the first name in big letters, about one-half inch high. He once said his test of size was that he needed to be able to read it from 20 feet away. He was cordial and friendly to all employees, whether they were old-timers or brand new, full-time or part-time.

One of his best forms of recognition was that he treated everyone as equals. He treated them all as if each and every one was a very important person. I don't know if he ever read Freud saying that one thing we all had in common was the "desire to be great." I don't know whether he read it, but he certainly practiced it.

I remember one time he invited me to follow him around a Wal-Mart store. He was greeting everyone—customers, employees —friendly to all. We then went back to the break room which was a little austere room about 10 feet wide and 15 feet long with vending machines taking up about one-third of the space and with a wooden table taking up about one-half the remaining space. Around this table were benches. When we arrived there, three or four employees were taking a break. They said hello-and didn't leave —a sure sign of good relationships.

Sam then asked the assistant manager to bring him the monthly statement. It was a beautifully simple statement showing the sales for the month compared with the same month of the previous year and expenses in about 20 categories compared to expenses the previous year. He then asked the people who happened to be in the break room how things were going. After listening, he referred to some of the numbers, saying such things as that he noticed insurance expense was up or something else was down. And he would ask them if they knew why. Some of them did!

Then something happened that I thought was amazing. He brought up what would normally be considered a management question. Should the store be expanded or should a new store be built down the road to handle the increased business?

Notice that this "management discussion" was instituted with the employees who just happened to be there at the time. One of them said that they needed a lot more space because business was picking up and they had put in some new merchandise. Sam said that he recognized that and he saw the point, but did they realize what it cost for Wal-Mart to have an empty store? He said they still had to pay the landlord for several years at a predetermined rate unless the store was leased to other tenants, and this wasn't always easy. Therefore, he asked, "Wouldn't it be easier to remodel this existing store?"

A lively discussion followed, and even though he was talking to working people, the discussion made as much sense (or maybe more) than if it had been held in many head offices. Wasn't this a wonderful form of recognition? In other words, he practiced what he preached. The employees were important people and they knew he recognized them as being important.

Another form of recognition I saw that day was his willingness to pose for pictures with Aunt Matilda or Cousin George or whatever employee or customer happened to be there at the moment. Just that one day he must have had 20 or 30 pictures taken with different employees. He always insisted that I get in the pictures. I have often thought that there must be many a mantelpiece in that small town, with pictures of Sam Walton and Aunt Matilda and some bald guy that remained unidentified.

Opportunity

There is an old Chinese proverb that goes something like, "One man's opportunity is another man's burden." Or, in Western terms, "What sounds good to one person doesn't do it for the next one." This difference creates many misunderstandings and often creates strains in relationships between management and employees.

One of the real all-time experts in the field of personnel relations is a man named Charles Hughes. He was, for many years, the personnel manager for Texas Instruments. He wrote an excellent book, *Making Unions Unnecessary*, as well as other books on related subjects. He points out that one of the most common mistakes was management assuming that if they thought something sounded good that the employees would feel the same.

Webster's says that an opportunity is "a situation or condition favorable to attainment of a goal." To some people the goal is advancement through promotion. To others it means advancement in skills and education. To others it means increased security. To others it sometimes means more money, although this is not as common as many managers think.

Although aggressive people have a hard time understanding this, there are millions of good, hard-working, valuable, conservative people who want only to continue doing what they are doing. They like what they are doing. They feel good about it. They often feel that what they are doing is very meaningful. They want the opportunity to continue doing it until they choose to retire. This type of person doesn't want someone else to tell him when to retire. They want the opportunity to continue to work until they are psychologically and financially ready to "hang it up."

What appears to be a good opportunity to one person may not be so to another. As Charles Hughes said, "What looks good to you as a manager may not look good at all to someone in the office or the factory floor." We managers often make the common mistake of assuming that we know what people want and what they would consider to be a good opportunity.

We had an interesting example of this with one of our best machinists.

Charlie was not only a good machinist, he was also a good "company man". He was always there on time, turned his work out with high quality and on schedule. He was also a good teacher to new and less skilled machinists. Therefore, we assumed that when the position of foreman of his department opened up, Charlie would be delighted to receive the promotion. So we promoted him.

During the first month after the promotion, Charlie began to look more and more tired and haggard. One day about 30 days after his promotion, he came in and told his boss that he had a serious problem that he wanted to talk about. He had a problem putting into words exactly what the problem was. He finally blurted out, "Can I get my old job back?"

We said that sure he could. He was still the best machinist in the whole department. Naturally he could get his job back, but why would he want to? Why would he want to take a cut in pay and a demotion? He said, "Simple. I haven't had a good night's sleep in thirty days."

Once he was assured he could get his old job back, he started to look more relaxed. He said he still would have one problem and that was what he was going to tell his family. They had given him a big promotion party and were proud of him. He didn't know how to break the news to them. He was determined to do so, however. We suggested that he tell his family exactly what he had told us. He said he would. He did, and he worked for many more years till retirement as a happy machinist.

We learned a lot from this experience. We learned that the magic word "ask" is a very important one here, as in most other situations. Subsequently, we had two or three experiences where we thought promotions were in order and that they would be logical and welcomed by the employee, but were turned down. In other words, we learned more and more that what appeared to be a great opportunity to management sometimes did not to the employee. In fact, for many years, we would say to ourselves, "Let's not do what we did to old Charlie in the machine shop." But, on the other hand, I think we all recognized that that was a success story in a way. It showed the other employees that opportunities are there for advancement, but that there are other types of opportunities as well that may be more attractive to some employees.

Will Rogers had a beautiful formula for success and happiness. When asked what was the "secret" for happiness, he gave the same answer as for the "secret" for success. He said it was to know what you're doing, be good at what you're doing, and love what you're doing.

One of the beauties of Will Rogers' excellent definition of happiness and success is that it applies to both ambitious and aggressive persons whose idea of opportunity is to be promoted and to advance, and it equally well applies to the more conservative (psychologically) person who wants to continue what he is doing.

Even the person who is perfectly satisfied will sometimes, after a few years, want to make a change. Management calls this a "lateral" change, but often this is exactly what the employee wants. This is where open bidding is very important. Many companies do not offer this opportunity for fear that they will lose skills.

Our theory is that you don't really lose skills when you allow someone to move. You give the employee the opportunity to add skills. The more skills that are added by employees, the stronger the company becomes. It also gives the company the ability to keep good, capable people. This is absolutely vital for success.

One of my mentors many years ago told me that you simply couldn't afford to lose a good employee. He said he would go so far as to follow them home if they were unhappy or were planning to leave the company. Most of us, including me, thought that this was just an expression, but he literally did that one time. He followed an employee home, discussed the situation over the kitchen table with the man's family present, and succeeded in having this employee stay with the company. It involved finding a more interesting job for this valuable employee, which was done. The man stayed with the company for many more years, doing a great job.

The word opportunity often conjures up money in the minds of many people. Amazingly enough, money, although an important factor, is not usually the top one. It is not even in the top three with many people. Some people say it is analogous to the price of a product. Everybody talks about it, but most people don't buy on price alone.

When money does become an issue, it can certainly become very "touchy". What is often the issue is not the absolute level of the compensation but the relative level compared to the employee's peers. Many an employee making X dollars was quite happy with his pay until he found out that his associate was making X plus a couple of thousand per year. It became even worse if he saw that someone whom he thought of as less valuable was making more.

Since good relationships are based on trust, pay scales that are perceived as being unfair are often perceived by employees as being a violation of this trust. Therefore, illogical or unfair pay policies can be very damaging to relationships. The fairness of the policies themselves are often more important than the pay level, unless the level is perceived to be unfairly low.

To some employees who have a good relationship with the company, whether it is a large company or a small one, opportunity means the chance to grow with the company. This is one situation where a small company that is growing rapidly has an advantage over a larger, slower growing company. The smaller company has a better opportunity to create the feeling that "as the company goes and grows, we all go and grow." In addition, a small company can often grow faster than a large ones.

Peter Drucker, in his book *Management: Tasks, Responsibilities, Practices*, discusses the advantages of small companies over large companies. He counters this with advantages of scale of large companies. He comes to the conclusion that "fair-sized" companies have the best of both worlds. Also, the fair-sized company can often provide more job security than the small company, which in itself is seen as an opportunity to many.

Steady Work
One of the best ways to have good relationships with employees is

to have what is known on the factory floor as "steady work." Where does steady work come from? Some people think it comes "from the company." Okay, that may be right, but it begs the question of where the company gets this work. Believe it or not, many times with highly educated people, as well as those not so highly educated, you have to ask three or four questions before the word "customer" is even mentioned. Amazing!

Steady work has an important and sometimes emotional meaning to most employees. To industrial engineers, it has a different, logical meaning. Since we are discussing building stronger and better relationships with employees, let's take what employees mean by steady work.

It means lack of layoffs. It doesn't necessarily mean never but it certainly doesn't mean frequent. Companies historically have used layoffs as a way to balance production to incoming orders. To many of their employees, whether the company knows it or not, this is considered unfair and to some, poor management. The word layoff itself is perceived as dirty, even obscene.

Realizing this, many companies nowadays use other words instead. One is "restructuring," which had a prior and more accurate use in financial circles. Or even more dazzling (or more accurately perceived as B.S. by the troops) is the new MBA goody, "re-engineering," Here again this word formerly had a different and more respectable meaning in other areas.

Unless economic conditions are extremely tough and unless other companies in the area are doing the same, layoffs to most employees are perceived to be due to failures by management. They ask, "Couldn't something have been done to avoid these damn layoffs? Or at least to make them less severe?" or "Couldn't we have gotten some new business or new products or something?"

Management often answers (or even worse, doesn't answer at all), "There's a recession going on" or "Nothing we can do about it." I feel the main reason for layoffs is poor relationships with customers; in other words, not enough business to sustain the work force and keep everyone busy. It is often as simple as that. Sure, there are other factors involved, such as underlying economic trends and recessions, but notice that really good companies seldom downsize or lay off people.

Actually several things can be done to avoid layoffs. *Fortune* magazine listed seven in their excellent article, "Is This Layoff Necessary?" (*Fortune*, June 1, 1992). Their answer was, "No, and it may even reveal stupid management." This article brings out the key point that layoffs are bad for everyone. They are bad for relationships with all three key constituencies.

Obviously layoffs are bad for employees. Trying to get a job during a period when companies are laying off is extremely difficult. Layoffs are not only bad for the ones who got the axe, but also for the others. Waiting for the next notice is no fun. As a senior vice president of Ford said, "The survivors become traumatized." It's like waiting for the other shoe to fall.

Right Associates in Philadelphia questioned 909 companies who had downsized (another buzzword) during the past five years. Seventy percent reported that workers who were spared felt insecure about their employers. This, of course, is not to be compared to the anguish of those without jobs. What does all this have to do with relationships? What does it do to relationships that may have previously been satisfactory? How long will it take to rebuild them?

Let's look now at how layoffs affect relationships with customers. One might think they would improve. Logically they could, but usually they deteriorate. Why? Several reasons. One is that people usually work best in teams. When the team is broken up, efficiency usually goes down—and so does quality quite often. Therefore, customers are often hurt two ways: lower quality and longer time.

Furthermore, who are such precise planners that they can accurately decide in a layoff who goes and who stays? If they were such good planners, they might not have gotten in difficulty in the first place.

We had an amusing, although not at the time, experience along these lines. During one of the most severe postwar recessions, we were having serious problems with a key supplier. Deliveries were coming slower and slower. Four weeks went to six, then to eight. Since it was a rapid change and an unexpected one (one could have thought the opposite) we were caught off-guard. Our customer service on products using this component was suffering. How could we explain to our customers this time deterioration, particularly in the middle of a recession?

We arranged a visit to their factory in New England. After a plant tour, which revealed a plant running about half speed, the general manager took us to lunch. He tried to be cheerful, but he really wasn't. He explained that they had experienced a few months back a sudden 40 percent decline in orders. He said, "This had never happened before." Then later he told us that headquarters had issued an edict for a 50 percent layoff. He had only half his previous workforce. We then saw why we were having problems.

We responded that there was a simple explanation of the recent decline in service to us, a good customer. We told him that he was in the position of being 20 percent oversold. "No," he said. "I'm 40 percent undersold." We pointed out that as far as a customer was concerned it was the same as if he had been running 100 percent production with orders coming in at 120 percent. They had, as many do, overdone their lay-offs.

He finally agreed with our point of view. He convinced his bosses using our logic, I later heard. Pretty soon service and deliveries improved. The long-term benefit was that the important relationship between us, which had been rapidly deteriorating, was repaired. It is now, after many years, stronger and better.

How about the effect of layoffs on relationships with shareholders? The CEO of Dow Chemical was once quoted as saying, "Layoffs are horribly expensive and destructive of shareholder value." I was quoted in the same *Fortune* article about the evils of layoffs: "We don't take this approach (resisting layoffs) just to be good guys, but to build a good company and get the best people." One reason I stated was the high cost of layoffs to the company. Experience has shown that, if and when laid off employees are recalled, the best 15 or 20 percent have taken jobs elsewhere. Naturally this depends on duration of the layoff—if it's a long one, losses are even higher and more costly.

When a company lays off experienced people, it is damaged in the same way that it would be with the loss of any other valuable asset. No doubt about it. A good, experienced, dedicated and well-trained employee is a very valuable asset.

How do you prove this to the person who says, "If you can't count it, it doesn't count?" Not easy. You know it's true, but how do you prove it? One approach is to add up the cost of recruiting and training a new employee. The amount and duration of training required to bring the new one up to the level of the experienced lost one is usually surprisingly high. This is particularly true if management time is added to the other costs.

Also the inevitable deterioration of product quality and service harms both the shareholders (owners) and customers. I once heard an expert industrial securities analyst say that if he could only secure a few facts about the company he was researching, yearly turnover of employees would be one of the key numbers. Does this mean that companies with lower employee turnover are more successful than their competition with high turnover? I have been unable to find research to prove this point. However most experienced managers that I've known feel strongly that a good workforce is an important competitive advantage.

To look at this from the employees' point of view, as to how productivity is affected, "When business is down, why should I work myself out of work?"

Fortune's list of ways to avoid layoffs included:

1. Plan ahead and curb new hiring when business is still pretty good.

2. Plan ahead and use overtime judiciously.

3. Just say, "No." Think of cost of retraining, loss of customer service and quality. Is it worth it?

4. Retrain and redeploy people—crosstraining helps.

5. Use voluntary leaves.

6. Shorten the work week. Employees call this by the positive phrase "work sharing." During one recession, which fortunately didn't last too long, we asked our employees what they thought we should do. This was the first time we had heard this phrase, "work sharing." It came from the employees. They told us they much preferred this over other alternatives.

7. Introduce new products (my addition to the *Fortune* list). Get new products ready to go and present them when they are needed and welcomed by employees. A new product which employees may consider a pain in the neck during boom times will usually be welcomed when things slow down.

Better Communications

Okay, everyone talks about good communication. What do we mean by this? To answer this I think we must look at what communications consist of. The obvious intent of communication is "for the exchange of information."

Also it can be said that another form of communication is that covered by the old saying that "Actions speak louder than words." On the factory floor, this is often expressed as, "He talks the talk, but does he walk the walk?"

Another important function of communication, in addition to conveying information, is to build better relationships. Therefore, our definition of "good communication" is that which does a good job of fulfilling both functions. First, to accurately convey information in a timely manner and second, and just as important, to help build better long-term relationships.

It has been proven many times that good communications depend on credibility. Credibility in turn is based on trust. Good relationships are also based on trust. Therefore, doesn't it logically follow that good communication is vital to good relationships? Or couldn't it be said that good relationships must have good communication to build and strengthen them?

There are many barriers to good communication. One of the least obvious but most common is the everyday aggravating and sometimes very frustrating use of ambiguities. Some people use ambiguities so often that one wonders if they are done, consciously or subconsciously, purposely or accidentally. At least the recipient of such ambiguous communication, particularly if it is of a repetitive nature, sometimes becomes suspicious of the sender. This suspicion is often based on "Take your pick of what I mean and then I will tell you later which was the right one after we find how things turn out."

Many other ambiguities are absolutely innocent. But even in the most innocent, when one asks what the sender meant, the sender almost always becomes somewhat aggravated and says, "You know what I mean." This puts the receiver on the spot of either guessing, dropping the subject or saying, "No, I don't know what you mean."

We had an amusing, but potentially expensive, example of this several years ago. At that time we were a small company, and rather poor. We had the opportunity to buy two high-quality Minster (used, but in almost new condition) punch presses. I was told, "We can buy them for $50,000." Fifty thousand dollars was considered a heck of a lot of money.

This brought up the obvious (at least to the receiver) question: "Do you mean $50,000 each or $50,000 for the two of them combined?" The engineers that told me about this could give me the model numbers, the serial numbers, the ages, the tooling, the weight, the capacity, and the die sizes, but they couldn't tell me whether the seller wanted $50,000 each or $50,000 total.

I suggested that they clarify this so we could see whether we could afford it. We could afford $50,000, but $100,000 was beyond our means. I was told that this would be "too embarrassing" or "if we asked they would naturally give us the higher number."

After some discussion we arrived at a simple solution. Simply write a purchase order describing these two presses in great detail and putting at the bottom a price of $50,000 total. Then if they meant $50,000 each they would come back and say so. Then we would have to say, "We pass." If they said nothing, we made a heck of a good buy.

They did mean total. We bought them. We used them for 20 years. In fact I think one of them is still running, and running well. The point of the story is kind of obvious. What sounded like a simple proposal actually had two meanings which were widely different. This situation was fraught with danger. Not only was $50,000 at stake, but relationships between sender and receiver (the seller and the buyer).

Some of the most frequently written "how-to" books on communication have to do with good listening. This is all very good. We should all be good listeners. However, what should we listen *to*? Most of the "how-to" listen books give little or no clue as to which questions to ask, or how to ask them. If you don't ask the right questions, how do you know if you are listening to something relevant?

Another reason for learning the importance of asking good questions is that many people have some great ideas that they don't volunteer. Sometimes these ideas are well thought out over a period of months, or even years, but they are still locked up in a person's mind, sometimes in a group's minds. To unlock them only requires a simple question; the type of question often starting with, "What do you think we ought to do about ...?" or "Does anyone have an idea about how we can go about solving this problem?"

We had an excellent example of this several years ago. The situation was that we were running three shifts, raising production as fast as we could. We had one large problem and a smaller one, both holding us back. The large one was that our second shift continually showed less productivity and lower quality than our first shift. The third shift was somewhere in between. We calculated that if we could build the second shift up to anywhere near the productivity and quality of the first shift, we could increase production to the extent that was needed at the time.

Our management people had several theories of why the second shift was not up to par with the first shift, but the theories didn't seem to work out in practice. It became apparent that the theories made sense to management, but not to those on the factory floor.

Finally someone came up with the right idea. I am embarrassed to say that we didn't think of it sooner. The idea was to ask the people on the factory floor what they thought could be done to solve this problem. We asked the second shift people first.

They said that they had a rather simple solution. A few more questions revealed that the solution they had in mind was well thought out, far from a half-baked idea. It was a simple idea, actually elegant in its simplicity.

They said all we had to do was change the times of the shifts. They said the reason the second shift was unpopular was that they had to come to work at 4:00 in the afternoon and were not able to leave until 12:30 at night. This meant that the older people were unhappy about not getting home until way after midnight, and the younger ones felt there was nothing to do around town beginning at 12:30 a.m. (For once the younger ones agreed with the older ones.)

We asked what we could do about that. They said all we had to do was to move the second shift up to start at a quarter till three in the afternoon, ending at a quarter till eleven. In other words, start 1 1/4 hours earlier than before. Then those who wanted could be home well before midnight, and those who wanted to go out could still bowl a couple of lines or grab a couple of beers. We said that made sense, but how would this solve the problem? They said that with these more favorable hours, we could keep a steady crew on the second shift. People wouldn't keep bidding off or leaving or trying to get on our first shift (or someone else's first shift).

We said this made sense, but how about the first shift? They answered us promptly that they had talked it over with the first shift people and it was fine with them. Since first shift were the early-birds, we were told that they were quite willing. Actually they would prefer to come to work at a quarter till seven and finish at a quarter till three leaving the rest of the afternoon for Little League with their kids or working around the house or taking care of cattle or horses. We checked with first shift, and sure enough, we found that a great deal of communication had been going on down on the factory floor between first shift and second shift. There was almost universal agreement that these hours would be much preferred by the employees and would help build up the second shift to be equal to the first shift.

Our secondary problem was that with 8 1/2 hours each on three shifts, this added up to 25 1/2 hours so we had a 1 1/2 hour overlap between the second shift and third shift. This was very awkward. They had this problem solved also. Have each shift in the building only 8 hours, therefore no overlap.

We then promptly pointed out that they were asking us to pay them while they were taking their half hour time for lunch or dinner. They said they had thought of this also and talked this over among themselves and would be pleased to trade that half hour for the two fifteen-minute breaks we had been scheduling. We then asked what would happen if some people wanted their breaks and the paid lunch both. That certainly wouldn't be fair to the shareholders ,or the customers either.

They said they had also thought of this and had discussed it. They said that if we would be willing to do this, they would police it themselves, to make sure that no one "cheated" on the break periods. If they wanted a coke or cup of coffee, they would bring their own.

We said we would try it to see if it worked. It did. It has been working ever since. The second shift did build up to be as good as the first. In fact, once they became a steady group without much turnover, they became as good if not better. Also the aggravating 1 1/2 hour overlap problem disappeared. In other words, it was a win-win situation all the way around.

What was this big success story based on? Good communications horizontally, but probably not so good vertically, was one verdict. In other words, while we didn't like to admit it, it appeared that the people on the shop floor were doing a better communication job than management and supervisors. Or possibly this was another Western Electric case, where management didn't know what the employees really wanted or were actually thinking. Ever since then our slogan has been, "When in doubt, ask" and "When not in doubt, ask."

As in building strong relationships with customers, face-to-face discussions with employees are vital to building good relationships.

When an employee feels he is not being treated right, or not being recognized, or not being appreciated, or simply wants to talk to someone about changing a vacation schedule or a hundred other things, is he going to talk this over with his computer? No! He wants to talk it over with someone who has knowledge of his situation, who will listen and, hopefully, understand.

Employee Surveys

One way of finding out what employees want and need is with employee surveys. Some surveys are excellent but some actually create negative results. The difference is apparent when you compare the two. The positive types ask questions that are relevant and answerable. The second type simply frustrates people. For example, to ask the employee if they work for a good company brings forth an answer from some of the brightest people something like, "I'm not a damn securities analyst. Those guys make a half a million bucks a year; why don't you ask them?" If the question is slightly modified to something like, "What do you think about the company?" or "How do you feel about it?" you'll get more of an answer. Or better still, make the questions more specific, such as, "How do you like our company's health insurance plan?" And have it graded on a scale from one to five or one to ten.

After a good survey form is developed, it is useful to compare what answers your company receives one year with those received the year before. The trend is often more important than the number itself.

We had a good example of that fairly recently when surveys showed that our health insurance plan was fading in popularity. We thought we had a great plan and were spending a lot of money for employee health. Instead of receiving applause, we were receiving rather low marks from the employees on surveys and also in personal interviews. We were typical management. We couldn't understand how when we had done something so darn good, it wasn't applauded.

One of the employees tipped us off when we were asking what was wrong. He challenged us to "Read the damn book and tell me what it says." Sure enough, the little book describing our plan, we found, was full of legalisms and medicalisms; sometimes even medical legalisms. Who could ever understand a medical legalism? Someone said, "You would need to be a Philadelphia physician to understand."

Therefore, we set about to improve our communications, the goal being to improve relationships. The more we read the book, this wasn't too hard to do. One of our people in the personnel department agreed to tackle the project, and she did a marvelous job. She cut down long words to short ones, long sentences to short ones, long paragraphs to short ones, and cut out irrelevancies. I should point out that she was not a medical or insurance expert. From this we learned to not have the creative, brilliant engineer write the instruction book on how to use the product he designed.

The net result was that the next survey showed that our health insurance plan was a heck of a lot better than a year ago. It was the same plan with some very minor changes. In fact, the actual changes were more on the negative side than the positive. Why the great increase in popularity? Better communications had to be the answer!

Open Door Policies

Another good form of communication, becoming increasingly popular, is the "open door." The only trouble with the open door is, according to lots of employees, it may be open but it has a trip wire attached to a booby trap. In other words, many employees are suspicious of an open door, feeling that you walk through at your own risk. The risk in many companies is chastisement from one's immediate supervisor, something along the lines of: "If you had such a big problem, why didn't you come to me with it instead of going to the big boss?" The answer is usually something along the lines of: "I tried, but I didn't feel anyone was listening." Therefore, to have a successful open door policy, it must be completely understood that no one will be chastised or penalized for going through the open door.

My favorite open door story is the one about the man who asked if he could see our company president. When he was invited in and asked what we could do for him, he answered, "You've already done it." He then smiled and said thanks and left. Draw your own conclusions. Mine is that he collected a bet upon his return to the factory floor.

Open door also means open telephone and open mail. I have received some of each from employees. Most of them bring up suggestions and/or complaints that are well thought out. Why then don't many bosses allow such direct communication? What are they afraid of? If they hear about a problem, it was there already. Isn't it better to have a problem that you understand than one you don't?

One anonymous letter from an employee at a branch plant far away saved us from a steadily deteriorating situation. Two points here. One was an illustration of the main point of this book, namely that as employee relationship started downhill at this plant, later profits followed downward. The second point was that "common wisdom" says to pay no heed to anonymous communication. This letter proved to be amazingly accurate. All four of his points turned out to be true. We acted upon all four of his revelations. Soon productivity and quality and morale improved; soon after, profits. That employee did us all a great service.

An open door policy has many benefits only if it is used sincerely and not as window-dressing. One is in problem solving. Many times employees have come in with a problem. When telling about it, they often start talking about possible solutions.

The extreme example, not unique, is where the employee states the problem, discusses options, solves the problem and then thanks the listener for all his help.

Discussion Groups

Another form of communication that is often very useful is informal discussion groups. These sometimes work well when management meets directly with the people in the office or on the plant floor without supervisors or middle management being present. This, of course, brings up the obvious problem of middle management being suspicious, at worst, or wondering, at best, what is going on in this meeting.

There is some risk here but the gain is usually worth it. For example, I can remember one time when I was at one of these communication meetings and was listening and learning a lot about quality improvement and ways to take better care of our customers. Everybody was participating well except an older lady who was obviously unhappy with the entire proceedings; perhaps with the entire world. This was noticed by everyone, including the personnel man who was moderating the meeting and asking questions. He then asked this unhappy lady if she had anything to add. As you might expect, when it came out, it came out as an explosion: "Do we really care about quality or do we just talk about it?"

Anyone who was daydreaming woke up fast. Unfortunately, she said this looking right at me. I asked her what she meant. She asked what to do when she, in the finishing line, had products come by that didn't look quite right to her, but looked okay to her associates and even to her foreman.

To even answer this was fraught with peril, only exceeded by not answering. The peril of answering, of course, was the risk of undermining her foreman who didn't agree with her concern. I had to think hard about this. I asked her how many people she was talking about. She said there were five of them that often thought the product looked okay when she didn't. I suggested that our customers were people too. If only 5/6th of them liked what we had shipped and 1/6th thought the product didn't look good, we would be running quite a risk of losing some customers. So I asked her what she thought we should do.

We ended up with a very constructive conclusion, that later got all around the plant. The conclusion was that anyone had the authority to speak up if the product didn't sound right, look right, or perform right. Several years later this became generally known as "empowerment." It works. Communications improve quality and improve customer service. Most important, working relationships improve. This is because such a good environment greatly lowers what many call the "hassle" factor. Also, most employees really want to do a good job, if they know what is considered a good job.

We see many examples of employees figuring out solutions to problems that management had struggled with for years unsuccessfully. One of our favorite examples was one cited earlier in this chapter about equalizing shifts in quality and productivity.

A much smaller example comes to mind but helps to make the point. We had two plants four hundred miles apart. One plant made parts for the other, and one shipped finished goods to the other, approximately a truckload a day in each direction. We had three drivers that took turns making these all-night runs over hills on a rather difficult road. It was hard work. We started getting a lot of complaints from the drivers, and even their families, about the layover at the other city while waiting for the load to come back in the other direction. Also, our accounting people noted that the expenses kept rising as the usual "Motel 6" got a little stale to the drivers, after spending many months driving the same route every night.

When we finally got around to doing the right thing, namely asking the drivers if there was a better way to do this, two of them right away said, "Sure, there's an easy way to make the company happy, save a lot of money, and make all us drivers happy at the same time." Naturally we asked what the solution was. They said it was "Simple." They were right; the solution was simple.

Their solution was to meet at a halfway point for dinner around midnight (they usually met and had dinner at this same place anyway), then switch trailers, turn around and go back home. This way they weren't out lying around a motel all day waiting for a load back. Their families were happier and our accountants were happier. Turnover went down, as well as expenses and complaints. This system has continued to work very well in the many years since.

Meaningful work, steady work, recognition, better communications are all important in improving and strengthening relationships with employees. There is another very important factor which is difficult to define. Employees sometimes call this "knowing what's going on." More subjectively, it may be "being in on things." Perhaps it is a feeling of what I think the psychologists call "belonging." This is the feeling that one is part of something, a part of a group or team. Also, the desire to, hopefully, be part of a winning team.

Education And Training
In the past most people thought of company sponsored education and training as being of benefit only to the company. Employees usually don't agree. Whether it is skills training, tailor-made to help the employee do his job better, or whether it is basic education, tailored toward the employee's improving his reading, math, and writing skills, most employees perceive this as a benefit to

them personally. If you look at both points of view, it is generally a win-win situation. If this is the case, and it appears to be with companies who have really studied the benefits why is education and training not offered more widely? Why don't all companies have some sort of training program for work skills and an education program extending beyond that?

Where can a company receive a better return on its investment? Note please that we are discussing this as an investment, not an expense. The accounting profession doesn't view it this way, though. They should. Robert Reich, who was Secretary of Labor in the Clinton Administration and a lecturer at Harvard for many years, has promoted the idea of what he calls "human capital." He says it is often a company's greatest asset. Therefore, it should be treated as such. What he calls "the arcane accounting profession" does not give this asset any credence or value. Therefore, they do not feel training and education of employees is indeed an investment.

One reason that training and education have not been considered investments by the financial community is that some of our most important assets are not readily measurable or amortizable. In the case of training and education, it could be contended that the investment itself is readily measurable, namely the out-of-pocket expenses such as computer programs, textbooks, teachers, classrooms, etc., plus the time expended. When it is stated that time may not be part of the costs, the accountant or measurer could be reminded that almost all manufactured products include time as part of the total costs. This is carefully and easily measured.

And then the argument is made that even if the investment is measurable, how could it be amortized? There are many formulas, of course, about capital expenditures, as to length of life, depreciable life, etc. This has been pretty much standardized. Accounting dogma says that human capital (as Robert Reich calls it), or training and education expense, is not as readily depreciable or amortizable.

Actually, there is a simple way to do this. That would be to calculate the average length of time of employment of those being trained and educated. If the average length of service of this particular group of people is fifteen years, why not amortize the investment over that period of time? Or if the company has rapid turnover, say 25 percent per year, then amortize it over a four-year period. If 10 percent, over a ten-year period. The argument here in favor of that idea is that low turnover would certainly increase the value of the education and training to the company making the investment. As one cynic put it, "I don't want to educate these people to the benefit of the next person who hires them." In any event, it can be done. I believe it will be done in the next few years.

Even more controversial is the attempt to calculate return on investment. To do this, of course, the benefits of training and education need to be estimated. This is difficult, but not impossible. There are a few companies that have made attempts to measure return on these investments. Motorola and Xerox are among the best known in education and training. Motorola claims their returns on investment far exceed returns from other investments; also, they exceed the returns they expected when they initiated these programs.

These returns are important. Even more important than the obvious benefits, certainly from a relationship point of view, is the feeling that employees have for the company that is offering education to them.

Ten years ago, we found that in most of our plants the reading level was about at the national average. We also found that the national average was not adequate for modern industrial needs. As Barbara Bush told us fifteen years ago, and it has since proved to be right, almost one out of three American adults could not read and comprehend what they were reading at the eighth grade level or higher. Despite many denials, especially from primary and secondary educators, this has proven to be true. We in industry can certainly attest to this.

New manufacturing methods, particularly flow types, are becoming more and more widely used. These are sometimes known as "employee directed." Instead of receiving verbal instructions from supervisors and foremen; instructions on what to make, when to make it, and how to make it, are given to the employees in writing. This is an important step in the widely used new buzzword "empowerment", although I prefer to think of this as an employee relationship improver. The old idea of going to the foremen to ask what to do and when to do it, in psychological terms, puts the employee and supervisor in what is known as the child-parent relationship. As one employee told me years ago, "It reminds me of when I was a teenager, before I had my own car, when I had to ask Dad for the car keys."

After an investment on our part in classrooms, teachers, textbooks, curriculum, and computer software to teach basic education and particularly reading, we received some amazing testimonials.

First, we found right from the beginning that the best way to present this to employees is to "Tell it like it is." The "is" is that this improvement in reading skills and comprehension is necessary for the company to do better. Or, as we told our employees, we must be competitive in world markets or we have no reason for existence. To be competitive, we must learn and use these new manufacturing methods, which if properly done will improve productivity, costs, quality, and customer service. This would require more emphasis on reading, math, and reading comprehension. Presented this way we usually received good cooperation from employees. In one of our smaller plants, on the other hand, the plant manager took it upon himself to present this as a "do-gooder" project, strictly for the good of the employees. As you would expect, he received less cooperation and a lower level of results.

Among the many testimonials we have received, one that comes to mind most clearly was when two employees came in together to tell me and a couple of my associates how much they appreciated our reading program. They said that it had improved their home lives as well as their work lives. One of them said he had two teen-age boys who were about to drop out of high school, wouldn't do their homework and wouldn't even discuss school. When he took his homework home, which of course is an important part of our reading course, he and his sons sat together around the kitchen table and gradually started doing their homework together. The boys stopped talking about dropping out. This was two years ago. Since then one of them has already graduated at about the middle of his class, instead of dropping out, and the other is also doing well.

The other employee said he was now able to read bedtime stories to his two little daughters without "faking it." He even said that his six-year-old, whom he thought he was able to fool all these years by looking at pictures and making up stories, said one night, "Daddy, you are really reading this now."

One of two workers later said, "I just want to tell you this is the best thing the company has ever done for me." (Bringing to mind, as a manager, things we had thought were more important such as health insurance, profit sharing, etc.) He was quite sincere. Whereupon the second man said, "Hell, it is the best thing *anyone* ever did for me."

This reading program started one day as a result of some repetitive mistakes that had been made in this particular plant. The year was 1987. The situation was that some prototype orders for an important prospective new customer had been wrongly produced. There were a couple of simple mistakes caused by not reading the entire shop order. Not knowing the source of the problem, I was very aggravated. I visited the plant and demanded the plant manager show me what had happened, and assure me it would not happen again. The next thing I knew we were out on the shop floor among a couple of hundred employees busily working. He directed me to the two welders who had apparently not read the shop order or followed the customer's instruction. I recognized these two as being a couple of old-timers and good company employees.

Being a little nonplussed that these two good, loyal, long-time employees were apparently the source of the problem, I asked them if they hadn't had access to the order or information. They said they did. But one of them rather sheepishly said, "I have a little trouble reading."

The lightbulb went on!

That was an important day for our company. Right there on the shop floor, with the plant manager and a couple of supervisors and the welders and their associates, we decided that we should talk this over. Not knowing where to go from there, I asked all the people, "What do you think we ought to do about this?"

Between the several of us, we decided there were only three alternatives. First would be: "Don't worry about it and hope it goes away," and "hope we didn't lose too many customers." Everyone there, including the welders, agreed this would be a poor alternative. The second possible alternative was to test everyone and fire the non-readers. Nobody thought this was a good idea either, including the welders. Also, I didn't think this was a good idea because we would lose some very skillful and dedicated employees.

Trying to lighten up a little bit, I pointed out that we could hire some Harvard English majors who could read the orders, but that they would probably be lousy welders. I think everyone agreed with this. The third alternative was that all our employees would need to be able to read. This was agreed by all present, management and employees, then and there. We later determined that eighth grade level was the minimum point.

The result, several years later, was a big success. Not only did we achieve the tangible and desired result of better utilization of the new manufacturing systems—fewer mistakes, better productivity, better quality, faster response time, etc., but we also found a tremendous intangible side benefit; namely, stronger relationships between the company and these employees were built up quite rapidly. Two indications of this is that after this program was instituted, turnover went down and productivity and profit went up.

Another by-product of our early education and training campaign back in the late '80s and early '90s was the amazing amount of national publicity we received. We were featured on American Broadcasting Company's public service messages about improving literacy. This ran on prime time many times. We were the feature of a *Fortune* article "The Three R's On the Factory Floor", and received many other accolades. This by-product had a very good effect on our image and reputation with customers, employees, and very often mentioned to us by investors and shareholders. Many of us lamented that some of the great things we had done, at least great in our own minds, had received very little recognition, whereas this relatively easy and pleasant literacy program received great recognition.

As a member of the Governor's Commission on Adult Literacy in our state, (appointed by Governor Bill Clinton after my complaining about the fact that we weren't receiving much help from the state), I had the privilege and the chore of speaking to many industrial leaders about literacy in the workplace. One of the most common excuses for lack of action was that they didn't know where to go for help. We were able to show several bosses that help in literacy is where you find it. Where you find it appears to be different in different areas.

In some areas community and junior colleges are of great assistance. In other areas, community colleges do not feel this is their responsibility. Some communities have public school systems with very efficient adult education programs and excellent teachers. In other areas, the votech people are very helpful, even though their primary mission is in skills training and vocational education. As we advised many people, the best thing to do is shop around and find the best help you can get, and then go to it.

To simplify the problem, in recent years, there has been some excellent software available for testing and teaching; some just as simple as playing video games, such as the "touch screen" type. There are also some excellent textbooks. There are good volunteer teachers out there. It is just a matter of looking for them and finding them.

There are other areas for education and training which not only improve companies and strengthen them competitively in the marketplace, but also greatly improve employee relations. One of the best areas for this is in quality training. After going through a whole series of quality training, also in the late '80s, we made some good progress, but ran into some opposition.

We found the opposition to be mostly logical. The fact that we were receiving feedback from employees at all was very encouraging, some of the feedback being positive and some negative. The negative feedback had to do with some feeling or hunch on the employee's part (which turned out to be mostly true) that there was a lot more to getting the job done than quality alone.

This led to the use of the Baldor Value Formula for employee training. The employees themselves grabbed hold of the formula, and formed their own five teams to write the five parts of the curriculum. We ended up with a homemade, but very professional curriculum, covering the entire subject of value. The whole curriculum was built around the idea of how employees can help increase value to customers, and in turn help the company and themselves. Once good relationships with employees are established, it becomes more and more clear to them that the company's prospering is to their benefit. In any event, this curriculum, designed by our employees, has turned out to be very successful. It is now being presented to all of our employees, everyone in the company, from top to bottom.

The curriculum is also being taught by employees. The talents that are there on the shop floor and in the corners of offices and laboratories are often not used. These talents, when uncovered, are constantly amazing to the careful observer. They were there all the time. This brings up the obvious question of why they aren't used. The word "used" is often taken as a negative, whereas our experience is that people love to have their talents recognized and, generally, enjoy using these talents. My father said many times, "I don't mind being used as long as you use me for a good cause."

I think it amazed many of us to see machinists and accountants become excellent teachers, doing a good job, presenting a part of the curriculum. This is good for relationships all the way around.

Profit Sharing

It is a popular concept for companies to promote "entrepreneurial spirit" and "feelings of ownership". How better can this be done than by providing ways for employees to *become* owners or, next best, to share in the profits?

Why not provide both opportunities? Employee stock purchase plans and profit sharing plans, not necessarily one or the other, work beautifully together. They promote reality of ownership and feelings of entrepreneurship.

There is a very practical side to profit sharing and stock ownership. After our profit sharing plan was instituted years ago, it became quite common to hear one employee say to another, "Your running up the phone bill is hurting my profit share," or on the factory floor, "Look at that barrel of scrap. What is that doing to our profit share?" Although this is often said in a good-natured way or in jest, it is generally quite well understood by the receiver that the sender is really trying to make a point. And a very good point from the company's point of view.

In recent years many profit sharing plans have been expanded to allow and encourage the employee to choose how this money will be invested. Since the best profit sharing plans allow the employees' money to stay in the plans untaxed, it allows the employee's money to grow much more quickly than it would on an after-tax basis. Therefore, how to invest the earnings year by year becomes increasingly important. One popular way to do this, and one we have done quite successfully, is to give the employee four choices. One of the four is in the company's own common stock, one in bonds, one in guaranteed insurance contracts, and one in a good equity fund. The employee has complete freedom to invest a portion in each or all in one and to change his mind once or twice a year. Profit sharing plans can work in conjunction with 401(k) savings plans.

A while back a very efficient switchboard operator who had been with the company for many years resigned to get married. Her husband did not want her to continue working. She withdrew her profit sharing when she left the company. She returned to visit a month or two later and was showing her former fellow employees several pictures. Knowing it was too soon to be showing baby pictures, I was curious, as were others, as to what the pictures showed. They showed a nice looking home. Our ex-switchboard operator was telling her friends in the office that her profit sharing had enabled her and her new husband to buy this new home.

She then apologized for interrupting the people's work. We, of course, told her to go ahead. We realized that there was no better illustration of the tangible benefit of a profit sharing plan than the ability to buy a new home. I have heard of other former and retired employees who bought ranches, invested in businesses for their children, and funded college educations with the proceeds from their profit sharing.

One last benefit I will mention of company profit sharing plans is intangible. Profit sharing promotes a feeling of belonging, as one young employee put it, "being a part of the action."

The cynics, who are wrong here, as they often are, said there are too many risks associated with having a profit sharing plan. One of the risks in profit sharing, they said, is what do you do when you have a bad year. This has happened to us, fortunately only one or twice. In both cases the employees understood much better than the cynics would give them credit for, that it had not been a good year and the profit sharing was less than the previous year and probably less than the coming year. This proved to be true. No problem. The understanding among employees was amazingly good and showed they understood the concept of profits, where they come from and how they are earned.

This brings up one of the very best benefits of profit sharing to the company, namely the opportunity that profit sharing gives for discussing free enterprise and capitalism. How do we make profit? Where does profit come from? What do we need to do to increase our profits? This benefits customers in that it shows the importance of customers to employees and also benefits shareholders. It shows that better profits come from better customer service and expense control.

Another very powerful way to create feelings of ownership, in fact actual ownership, is with stock options. For many years stock options have mainly been used for top management. A few years ago options became more widely used, but still mainly in the management area.

When we brought up the idea several years ago of issuing options to all employees with a certain length of service, we suggested five years or more; to cover the real career people. We were told that this was legal, but unconventional.

We found this to be not exactly true. It is done quite infrequently, but it can be done, and is done. Therefore, we decided a couple of years ago to start a stock option plan for all employees with at least five years or more of service. We were warned again by "experts" that this would be difficult to explain to people on the factory floor. To our pleasant surprise, as has happened on other subjects, the employees not only understood the program, they embraced it! It has gone so well that it makes one wonder: why don't more companies do this?

Employee Myths And Misconceptions

Just as in dealing with customers, companies often hold misconceptions or believe in myths that get in the way of building good relationships with their employees.

MYTH I:
You can't teach an old dog new tricks.

Wrong! This expression has probably caused more damage to free enterprise than any except "Build a better mousetrap and they'll beat a path to your door." We have proven that older people learn just as rapidly, sometimes more rapidly, than young people.

We had a good opportunity to study this when we worked hard for several years on basic education improvements. We found that the fifty-year-old nonreaders learned just as fast as twenty- or thirty-year-old poor readers. This surprised some of the teachers, most of whom had experience teaching children, not adults. Further, the teachers were amazed at the rapidity of learning. The old rule of thumb said it took 200 hours of teaching for each grade level advancement in reading ability. Several of our employees came up three grade levels with this amount of teaching.

The myth of the old dog and new tricks seems to be firmly implanted in many people's minds. It is simply not true and must be rooted out if the company is to secure maximum benefit from training and education. The maximum benefit is, of course, the ability of the company to become stronger, more competitive, and able to handle modern processes.

There is an old proverb that goes something like: "The man who is too old to learn was probably always too old to learn."

MYTH II:

Only educated people can learn complex jobs.

Wrong! Education is good. It helps a person succeed, as does intelligence, ambition, native ability, people skills, and other factors. But it is not a necessary condition.

We have had numerous examples. One of our best CNC (computer numerical control) machine operators was so good at his work that he became an unofficial teacher to other employees. Later he became an official teacher. He knew more about the complex and demanding processes of changing setups, to machine different parts of many hundreds of varieties, than most of the people employed by the machine builders.

He was what you would call a whiz. There was nothing he couldn't do with numbers. A couple of years went by. The man was doing great work not only for himself but helping other employees. He then came to us one day and asked if he could sign up for one of our Basic Literacy classes. We were surprised and wondered why such a successful, intelligent person would want to sign up for Basic Literacy. He took the basic test and, to our surprise, he proved to be (as he said) a third or fourth grade level reader.

He wasn't surprised. He told us he had never really learned how to read. I believe he said that only one other person in the world knew about this handicap. We as his employers certainly didn't. I don't believe his peers on the shop floor did either.

Once again, to prove his intelligence, he rapidly absorbed the instruction that he received in our reading classes. He rose from grade to grade with remarkable rapidity.

He became proficient enough to enter classes toward earning a General Equivalency Degree (GED). He did this also in record time and with flying colors. He then signed up for community college courses. This was within three or four years of the time he started his basic reading at the third or fourth grade level. He is now a teacher for others with reading and/or language difficulties. He is considered, as you might guess, one of the best teachers of all and has won many local and state awards. I once introduced him to one of our United States senators on a plant tour as, "The man who is on television even more than you."

The story is one example of an uneducated person who had the basic intelligence and native ability to master complex tasks successfully and responsibly. Certainly formal education is a great asset, but not a requirement, as this gentleman proved.

MYTH III:

Pay is the employee's number one concern.

Many managers answer the question, "What do workers want from their jobs?" with "Higher wages." While most inexperienced management people think this is true, it has been proven over and over to be definitely untrue.

The old original Western Electric, Hawthorne, New Jersey, study way back in the early 1900s showed that what management people thought workers wanted from their jobs and what workers actually wanted, were entirely different. A generation later, in 1949, the Lawrence Lindahl study published in *Personnel*, "What Makes A Good Job?" proved very similar. Same with studies made since. The Lindahl study which was very detailed covered ten factors that workers want from their jobs. Management said that "good wages" was the most important to the worker. The workers themselves ranked it number five, right near the middle. Of the nine factors in the Western Electric study, wages came out exactly in the middle: half more important, half less important.

Even more shocking is that in both studies (and subsequent studies have pretty well borne this out) what the workers listed as most important came out a sorry number eight by management in the Lindahl study. This was "full appreciation for work done."

To show this wasn't a fluke of misunderstanding, what the workers ranked as number two to them came out at the bottom, at number ten for management. This is the very important one of "feeling of being in on things."

Misunderstanding continued. Point three on the most important list for the employees came out number nine for management: "sympathetic understanding of personal problems." In all fairness, there were two factors which came out pretty close. "Job security" ranked number four and number two. "Interesting work" ranked number six and number five.

This bears out something that we have observed many times personally, namely that people on the factory floor, or the warehouse, or on the service desk are usually a heck of a lot smarter than their bosses think they are. It appears that the more inexperienced and more educated the boss is, the wider the gap between their opinions and reality.

One is often reminded of the most basic truths at times when basic philosophy is least expected. One time I was entertaining a couple of visiting customers at a local bistro. Down our way they are called beer joints. It is one of those nice old places where the booths are divided by partitions so that one can hear what's going on next door, but not see the participants.

There were three working guys in the next booth. It became clear right away, without a great amount of eavesdropping, that two of them were employees of our company and they were trying to convince the third one to "come over with us." Several interesting points were made. One thing that was particularly interesting to me was what was not discussed. Pay. I think towards the end of the discussion it was mentioned briefly, but not as a major point.

The major point they were making was the point of "steady work." One of them said, "We haven't had a layoff since I can't remember when." They also made a point about the freedom to move from job to job, or bid for open jobs. Another said, "You've got to work hard, but they treat you right." There was also a point made about, "I like to make something right and see it run and know it is going to do a good job out there" (meaningful work).

I told our personnel manager the next day that they did a better job of telling the strong points of our company than we did in our employee handbook and official publications.

MYTH IV:
Higher pay and better benefits will solve the problem.

The corollary to the previous myth is that when employees are dissatisfied, the thing to do is offer them more money or more fringes. This usually doesn't work. As previously pointed out money isn't the big dissatisfier that management often thinks it is. If pay or fringes are far below what their peers in the area are receiving, employees will object and will bring it up as a more important point. However, most successful companies, even moderately successful ones, pay reasonable wages and have reasonable fringes. Therefore, money is usually not the cause of dissatisfaction that management often thinks it is.

I remember one incident where a manufacturer was experiencing deteriorating employee relations. He knew it, but he didn't know the reason. It turned out later that the reason actually had nothing to do with money or fringe benefits. Not knowing this and thinking that throwing some money at the problem would solve it, he decided to add one holiday each year to the existing ones. This was done for about five years; he even added birthday holidays and Presidents' Day. When he ran out of holidays and stopped doing this, the next year there was a furor among the employees because they didn't get their new holiday.

The employer was nonplussed and a bit angry. He said things like, "Don't those dumb SOBs know how good I have been to them?" Actually, no, they didn't.

He found himself the victim of the "jelly bean effect." The name arises from the behavior of bears in Yellowstone Park. For several years there have been large signs warning people against feeding the bears. The reason does not have much to do with nutrition. It has to do with the fact that bears are good beggars and actors. They often beg for food, particularly sweets. They will be very good natured if you feed them a jelly bean or piece of candy, but if you run out of jelly beans it has been said that the beggar will try to remove the giver's arm.

MYTH V:

If it sounds good or feels good to me, the employees are going to love it.

Often not true. Some of the experts even say, usually not true.

Charles Hughes, in his milestone book, *Making Unions Unnecessary*, goes so far as to say to management, "If it feels good to you, don't do it." He is referring, of course, to policies involving employees.

MYTH VI:
Employees are "labor."

As far back as I can find, the textbooks in university business schools, particularly in accounting, refer to employees other than management and their cost as "cost of labor" or sometimes just "labor." When management refers to their employees as "labor," the company probably does not have good relationships with their employees.

What an employee is called is important. To refer to employees as "labor" is absolutely wrong! Who wants to be called "labor"? Or as I often ask management people, "How would you like to be called `overhead' or `burden'?"

Many times in accounting you see terms "direct labor," "indirect labor," "overhead as a percent of labor." On the factory floor or on the retail floor, the word labor to employees is not only a put-down but, even worse, often associated with union membership, even today when unions are usually not present.

This brings up an interesting question of what do you call employees. What is wrong with calling them employees? Sam Walton gave this a lot of thought and referred to all Wal-Mart's employees, whether full-time or part-time, as "associates." Some of the steel companies refer to "team members" and some others refer to employees as "partners" (a little dangerous, because it implies a legal meaning as well). But of course any of these are much better, for good relationships, than "labor."

We were having a management seminar at a nice resort. One evening we were discussing this important subject of employee relations. There was a very bright young waiter serving us. I noticed he was listening to every word even though he was only about high school age. He had all the looks of a winner. He was listening to this conversation between pouring cups of coffee and hustling drinks. So I asked him, "What do you like to be called?" Without a moment's hesitation, he said, "Star!"

One of my most vivid experiences with what "not to do" for employee relations occured a number of years ago when I visited one of our foundry suppliers. We were waiting for one of the owners who was out in the shop yelling at some of the employees. Much to our surprise, he was particularly berating a very large man that looked like a pro football linebacker. He picked up a shovel and threatened this very large man and told him in no uncertain terms to go to work someplace else. This was a bit shocking to me because I had seldom seen anyone treat an employee like this. I was surprised that his partners didn't seem shocked at all.

We then all went out to lunch and the man with the shovel was lamenting the "fact" of how hard it was to get good employees. I think his exact words were, "You can't get good labor around here." At the same time other companies, including ours, had long waiting lists of qualified employees waiting for work.

Crises In Employee Relationships

There are several different events which can cause minor or even major crises between a company and its employees. These events can either damage relationships with employees or can be opportunities to strengthen the relationship and benefit the company.

Technological change, as discussed in the customer chapter, is a potential hazard to almost any manufacturing or service business. One of the best protections against the hazards of technological change is having some good employees with their "ears to the ground" or their ears to the customer.

There is an old saying in army officer training that goes something like: "Don't worry when the troops are bitching, but if they are quiet, look out." The same with employee relations. When employees are coming up with ideas for improvement or even complaints for improvement, these are not only great opportunities for relationship improvement and strengthening, but are far, far better (although sometimes temporarily aggravating) than no feedback or no response.

The attempt of a union to organize a company's employees is a significant crisis in employee relations. Attacks by union organizing groups against nonunion companies can be among the most emotional crises a company and its employees may ever face. Tempers usually run high, claims and counterclaims are repeatedly made, and the federal government is involved whenever an election is called or when claims of unfair labor practices are made.

The outcomes of such traumatic clashes are usually predetermined by the strength, or lack thereof, in relationships between the employees and the company that existed before the union began attempts to organize. On several occasions there have been attempts to unionize employees at one of Baldor's plants. I have personally fought against such attempts, feeling that the best relationship between the company and its employees is a direct one—one not mediated by a union.

Whether a company has a union or not is, of course, up to the employees. The employees have a choice both legally and ethically. We always felt, however, and many others do also, that the most successful relationships are those when all work closely together—taking care of customers—without the interference of outsiders or a third party. We've always emphasized that steady work, pay and profit sharing actually come from customers, not from any union.

We had an interesting, amusing, and tense experience during one of these union organizing campaigns. The union, which was strong, extremely unscrupulous, and smart, had claimed that they could promise steady work to our employees. We had been stating in rebuttal that steady work comes from customers. We found later that this emphasis on where does our work come from, and who can guarantee that it will continue, became very important in our employee relations, as well as customer relations. There was one crisis during a final speech management was making prior to a union vote when we decided to run a bit of a test and, at the same time, continue our correct claim that business and steady work and orders come from customers. We asked the question: "Do you see the union buying many of our products?" Fortunately, and to our relief, about 60 percent of our employees laughed and some of the others frowned and some others looked puzzled. This was a good predictor of the election outcome and was quoted many times later.

Conclusion

Good companies almost always have good employee relations. Some knowledgeable people think that is pretty much the definition of a good company—namely a company where people like to work, where they feel they are respected as human beings, where they feel they can contribute to the good of the team, and be a part of the action and on a winning team. Good employee relations are vital for success.

OWNERS

Introduction

Good, long-term relationships with owners and shareholders are
extremely important, just as important as those with the customers
and employees. Whether we are talking about one owner who is also
the manager of a small business or a midsize business with fifty to
one hundred owners or a giant corporation with a million shareholders, all these different types of owners have one thing in common. It is a very important thing. They are all people. Therefore,
they wish to be treated as people should be, same as we have discussed previously regarding customers and employees.

People want to be treated right. By right I mean they want to be
treated with respect, told the truth, kept informed, and most important, treated as if they are important. Also, of course, they want
good results. In other words, they want to make money. They want
to participate in success. Much has already been written by others
about results, so we will stick with relationships—their importance
to success.

Sure, without good returns on their investments, shareholders will
eventually leave, regardless of how they are treated. However, good,
consistent, honest communications and fair treatment, with good
results, will lead to good long-term relationships. These encourage

shareholders to be much more patient and understanding in the face of adversity. Combined with good customer and employee relationships, this will, in the long run, produce good results for the company.

Or to put it in other terms, when good relationships are enjoyed, temporary bad news is correctly viewed as temporary in people's minds. Their patience then gives time for successful counter-measures to take effect. Then relationships become stronger than ever.

Relationship investing is a term that has begun to come into use recently. It has sometimes been linked with one of the all-time champion shareholders, Warren Buffett. As with many of Buffett's basic beliefs, this is based on an old commonsense fundamental; namely, that long-term shareholders want to build solid and close relationships with their companies.

After Baldor went public, one of our new and very successful shareholders was a firm believer in this fundamental. He didn't use the word "relationship," but he lived it. He talked to several of our customers, some salespeople, and many employees. He did this before investing and after, as well. His questions to all three groups were similar and all relationship oriented. These questions included, "How do they handle problems?"; "Do they stand behind their products?"; and "Do they tell the truth?" He was very successful. Why don't more investors do this?

Balance

There is a school of thought that says that the management of a company should favor shareholders over employees. For example, Nell

Minow, of Lands Incorporated, a Washington investment fund that describes its goal as "using shareholder rights to make changes in poorly performing companies", was quoted in the Wall Street Journal as saying that she would rather see management concentrate on pleasing shareholders than employees. She said, "The only way the system can work is if you make a long-term commitment to the people who provide the capital. If your goal is to make your employees happy, don't go to the public market for money, run a collective. When you go to the public market for money, you are a trustee for the shareholders."

No one can argue about the importance of being a trustee for the shareholders, but if the employees were to perceive that they were being treated as second-class citizens, compared with shareholders (or any other group), wouldn't shareholder value eventually suffer, and suffer greatly?

Further rebuttal to the school of thought which says that the company should favor shareholders over employees was illustrated by a recent experience with one of our largest shareholders. This gentleman is extremely intelligent, well-informed, and quite a powerful man on Wall Street. He tends to be critical of "his companies." He, like many shareholders, rightly thinks of Baldor as his company.

In previous conversations with this gentleman, discussions centered around numbers; such as earnings per share, quarterly, annually, projected growth, etc. Shortly after *Fortune* announced the "Top 100 Companies to Work for in the United States" he called and said he was absolutely delighted to see Baldor included in this list. He was quite effusive, which surprised me as all of our previous conversations had been more in the "left-brain" area. I pointed this out to him and he immediately rejoined, "Hell, it takes good employees to get good numbers, doesn't it?" Well said!

Chrysler Corporation, in their 1995 annual report to shareholders, stated it very well. They supported the concept of the importance to a company of working to earn good relationships with shareholders by striving for good relationships with customers, suppliers and employees. Chrysler's Annual Report stated, "We know that the best way to serve our shareholders is to first serve our customers. And we know that our shareholders won't be served unless our employees are inspired and unless our dealers and our suppliers are partners in the enterprise." Well said!

Among the leading exponents for many years of treating the shareholder well, sometimes to the detriment of the employees, were some of the old-fashioned financial institutions. Many of them, and this is mostly past tense, treated the shareholders like kings and the employees like pawns. You don't see that much anymore, which either means that they learned and adapted, or went out of business.

Without using the word "balance," Marshall Loeb, long-time publisher of *Fortune*, expressed it very well. He said, quoting Frederick Reichheld in his book, *The Loyalty Effect*, "The message is simply this: The best, most profitable employers are those that inspire loyalty among three constituencies: customers, investors, and employees." Note that Mr. Loeb, quoting Mr. Reichheld, does not favor or emphasize the importance of any one over the others.

What Owners Want

Much has been written about the differences between shareholders/owners—large versus small. Certainly the 100-share stockholder in Montana is different from the 100,000-share buyer and portfolio manager on Wall Street. One is probably an amateur investor while one is certainly a professional. One is probably investing a portion of his savings while the other is making investment decisions for other people and his performance can, and will, affect his entire career.

Since so much has been written about the differences, possibly it is more productive to talk about what they have in common. This would also apply to owners of any business whether it is a small partnership or a working interest in an oil well or shares in a publicly traded company. What do these people have in common?

One, they want to make money. Some short term, some long term, some small amounts, some large amounts, but number one, they all wish to make a profit.

Two, they all want to make good investments. This is true whether it is a "laugher," as part of a hobby, or part of a vital "to bet the company" decision. Another way of saying this is that people want to make good decisions. They want to be right. Investment decisions are particularly sensitive to analysis and second-guessing.

Three, investors want a certain amount of security. While all investors, large or small, realize that there is risk in all investments, one thing we all have in common is that we like to see the best prospects for gain with the least possible risk. We also want to feel we understand the risks we are taking.

Four, all types of investors want is to be told the truth. This has a left-brain side, a very logical one, and a right-brain side. The left brain side is, of course, that better information leads to better decisions. The subjective (right) side is that we all feel better with the truth. We particularly feel the need for better relationships. Truth leads to better relationships.

Five, in addition to being told the truth, we wish to be told all that we believe is relevant toward our making good decisions. Sometimes we get the truth but not enough to give us a feeling of security and the feeling that good decisions are being made. We want to be informed in a timely manner. We want to feel the information we receive is fresh and relevant. No other shareholders get a head start.

Six, probably the most difficult thing to explain but what we all want is the paradoxical but important feeling of consistency and change; consistency in important, vital subjects, such as integrity, commitment to building good relationships with customers, employees and shareholders, and commitment to being competitive; change in other important areas, including adaptability to changes in markets, response to new opportunities, and flexibility to accept and use new technologies. Maybe the most important of all is the willingness to change as people's needs and wants change.

Who's In Charge?

Who is responsible for building strong relationships with share-holders? Many companies delegate this task to outsiders, to firms specializing in shareholder relations. In the old days there were a number of firms in New York known for financial public relations. This gradually fell out of favor and now there are several firms that specialize in investor relations. Many companies who handle shareholder relations in-house do so through an investor relations department.

In many companies the CEO and/or the chairman handle investor relations. In others there are several people who are willing and able to talk with shareholders and securities analysts. Some of the best and most active securities analysts want to talk to not only the chairman and the president, but the chief financial officer, the head technical person, and in many cases the head of marketing. Some of the most successful analysts are anxious to talk to a cross section of management rather than just one person. They would far rather do this than talk to an investor relations department or a financial public relations specialist. In fact, many of them will not talk to anyone but a principal of the company itself.

Saying to the shareholder who has some questions or comments, "You will need to talk to the investor relations department," is analogous to the old-fashioned practice of telling unhappy customers that they would have to talk to the sales department, or worse, the complaints department; or to a quizzical or unhappy employee, that he or she would have to go to the personnel department. People react badly to being shunted aside. This is something else that employees, customers, and shareholders have in common. Because they are all people.

Communicating With Shareholders

Shareholders are people with wants and needs. Among the most important of these is the desire to be told the truth. This brings up the important subject of shareholder communications. Without good, honest communication with shareholders, relationships don't last long.

All long-term relationships are built on trust and trust is built on truth. The owners and shareholders want the truth and feel they are entitled to it. They want it so they can feel secure in their investments and also for their strong desire to feel that they are a part of the action. Objectively, whether they are small shareholders/owners or large ones, truth is needed by all of them so they can make better investment decisions.

This sounds pretty obvious. Apparently it isn't as obvious as it sounds, as this truth principle is often ignored or even perverted. It is often clouded by people asking, "So, what is the truth?" and "To whom should this be told?" or the old military-political saw, "Who needs to know?"

There are other reasons, or sometimes even excuses, for not telling the truth, such as, "If we tell these people, we will have to tell the other owners." The answer to this is, "Of course."

Another reason often given for not giving out news is, "If we tell this story, it will benefit our competitors." No one expects trade secrets to be made public, but wouldn't it be fair to ask, "Isn't this something that would also benefit the shareholders?"

One of the best at building good, strong shareholder relations was Sam Walton of Wal-Mart. Back in 1977 or 1978, our company and Wal-Mart and fourteen other midsize companies (it is hard to remember when Wal-Mart was midsized) were invited to Chicago to address the Chicago Society of Security Analysts. This was one of those programs where analysts signed up for the presentations they wanted to hear. There was a limit of twenty at each session (wisely limited to a small number so there would be more opportunity for interaction and questions). In turn each company agreed to put on three sessions of one hour apiece.

They put the sign-up sheets in the ballroom of the Palmer House. We were asked to standby in case there were any questions from analysts trying to decide which sessions they were going to attend. Sam's sign-up sheet was clear across the ballroom from ours. Suddenly in this decorous atmosphere—a three-or four-story ballroom in the old grand style—a whoop and a holler came across the floor. It was Sam. He came bounding up and said, "Guess what? The first two companies to be filled up are from Arkansas!" He was referring, of course, to Wal-Mart and Baldor.

Soon thereafter I heard several analysts speaking about why they wanted to go to Sam's presentation. It was pretty much along the lines of, "He tells it like it is," or "I've heard that he really answers questions." There is not any doubt that his expertise in shareholder relations was an important addition to his building great relationships with employees and customers. A few years later his company became the undisputed leader in its field.

Communicate Clearly

Another important principle in building good shareholder relations is right out of Dale Carnegie. Mr. Carnegie said 60 years ago that one of the fundamentals of building up good relationships is to put things in the other person's terms—in terms they can understand. Many companies have difficulties doing this. Some of the worst are the "high-tech" companies that think that everyone knows what an IGBT is or a vector drive or a CD-ROM.

At the time when we were getting ready to go public and doing what was known as "due diligence" (referring to the supposed diligence of the listener and questioner rather than the speaker or the answerer) we had an experience illustrating this. It was during the energy crunch of the mid-70s. We listed several competitive advantages that we thought were important. We thought others would think this too.

One of these competitive advantages had to do with our motors being more efficient than most of our competitors, thereby saving energy and money. We showed charts and graphs and thought we had really made this point very well. One gentleman standing at the back of the room was audibly and visibly not buying. He must have been an influential person because other people watched him. Later I found that he was a good guy, and that he was indeed influential.

Fortunately (although it seemed unfortunate at the moment) when it came to the question and answer session, this gentleman said something along the lines that he thought we were making too much of the efficiency differences over our competitors. He asked, "What is the difference of three or four points? What is the big deal?"

We had shown that motors use a tremendous amount of electricity to produce mechanical power. The old rule of thumb is an average of one dollar a day per horsepower. To run a 100 horsepower motor continuously around the clock costs about $35,000/year. It is pretty amazing to think that a $3,000 motor, total cost, could use 11 or 12 times its own cost in electricity in one year, but it can. This happens with average electricity rates and running the motor continuously, as they often do in process industries.

The reason I am explaining all this is that I thought I had explained it very well to the audience, namely the importance of the efficiency of the motor, due to the large amount of electricity consumed. Small differences in efficiency produced large dollar savings. I had made the near fatal mistake of thinking I got my point across, when I hadn't.

As old Dale Carnegie said, try to put things in terms that are familiar to the listener. After all those charts and explanations I had the experience of having a man doubting the importance of something I knew was very important. That was frustrating. Also I knew this was obviously a crisis situation. We were either going to come out ahead or way behind.

Remembering the old Dale Carnegie maxim, I tried a whole different approach. I reminded the man that our example showed a $3,000 motor and asked him if it were possible to buy a $3,000 automobile (that would run) and if we knew we were going to spend $35,000 per year for gasoline to operate this automobile, wouldn't a small difference in gas mileage be pretty important to him?

His response was, "Why didn't you say that in the first place?" This was accompanied by a couple of nods of his head and a bit of a grin. This was very reassuring. Even more reassuring was looking around the room and seeing other people nodding and understanding for the first time. The point is that it was obvious from my point of view, being in the motor business for over 20 years. However, I was talking to people who were extremely bright, intelligent, and well-informed, but who hadn't had much personal acquaintance with electric motors. I had obviously not presented this from *their* point of view.

Later, as I got to know this gentleman, we both chuckled about this experience. He confirmed what I had suspected, that my original explanation (which I had thought was excellent) had gone over (or under) many in the audience.

This experience illustrates in a way what is probably the second most common mistake in the relationship with shareholders. Obviously the most deadly mistake is to not tell the truth or to withhold the truth. The second is to tell the truth but in a way which is not readily understood by the listener or reader. We specialists often assume that our "lingo" is familiar to everyone. Not so.

In Dale Carnegie's original book, *How To Win Friends And*

Influence People he says if the reader only got one thing out of reading his book it should be, "An increased tendency to think always in terms of the other person's point of view and see things from his angle as well as your own.... If that is the only thing you get out of this book, it may prove to be one of the milestones of your career." Of course, this is easier said than done, especially when dealing with a heterogenous group of shareholders. One must try, however.

An example that sticks in my mind is what happened four or five years ago after one of our shareholders meetings. There was an elderly, white-haired lady who had been a shareholder for many years and had attended many shareholders meetings. She always listened attentively. To my recollection, she had never asked a question or made a comment.

One year she buttonholed me after the meeting and said in front of several other people that she had two questions. The first question was, "Mr. Boreham, aren't we doing pretty well in the motor business?" I said, "Yes, we are."

Her second question was, "Then why are we getting into the electronics business?" My life flashed before my eyes, because I thought we had covered that very well in our presentation. I thought we explained that we were augmenting our motor business with electronic controls rather than diversifying, as the question would infer. To have simply repeated what we had already said would have been insulting to this nice lady, so that was out. My next thought was to use some technical terms, but that would have been almost as bad. So that was out.

This left only one alternative which I have never used before and I replied, "Mrs. Blank, it is not that we are getting into the electronics business. The electronics business is getting into our business." Her face lit up and she nodded her head and she said, "You mean like my new washing machine with all those electronic controls?" I said, "Yes, ma'am, good example. And have you noticed that your new car has a lot of new electronic controls, more each year?" She said she had noticed that and that she understood and she came close to saying, "Why didn't you say that in the first place?" So why didn't I? Too simple. Not the way we were trained.

We had a situation one time where we thought we explained a new acquisition that we had made which greatly augmented our business. We thought we had explained it well. It turned out that we had made a good move, but had not explained it well. We drew little boxes showing our present business, and a separate box showing the new products, new markets, and new technologies acquired in the acquisition. We were talking augmentation but the picture we drew was of diversification.

We later found, and we should have known this sooner, that diversification was an unpopular idea among our shareholders. Many felt that we were going in the right direction originally and that diversification could be a risky and possibly unsuccessful thing to do. When we later found that shareholders felt this way, we returned to where we should have been in the first place, namely explaining that this was an augmentation not a diversification. The proper picture to draw then was of concentric circles rather than a box on one side and another box on the other side.

In other words, what we had done was ultimately well accepted by shareholders, but the way in which we explained it was not popular. When explained properly, the idea gained good acceptance.

As it is with employees and customers, arrogance is just as fatal here, perhaps even more so. "Talking down" to shareholders is just as bad, possibly even worse, than being incomprehensible.

I recently read of a major company that told its shareholders they were about to "re-engineer" their business to "add value" and to do this they were going to have a "paradigm shift." What the heck did this mean? How do you think the shareholders reacted to that bunch of "buzzwords" strung together? Were they saying that they were going to do a heap of cost-cutting or downsizing, or come up with new strategies or what?

One of the greatest experts of all times in handling the English language as it should be handled was Winston Churchill. One of the best stories about him was when an American top general once asked Prime Minister Churchill to look over a draft of a speech he had prepared. The general got a note back from Churchill saying, "Too many passives and too many zeds."

When the general asked Churchill to amplify and clarify his criticism, Churchill replied, "Too many Latinate polysyllabics like 'systematize', 'prioritize' and 'finalize'." Doesn't that sound awfully familiar?

Then he really polished off the general by saying, "What if I had said instead of 'We shall fight on the beaches...' that 'Hostilities will be engaged with our adversaries on the coastal perimeter?'

Yet, here we are 50 years later being inflicted with such words as "prioritize," or even worse "maximize," or worst of all "optimize." The last two really, upon analysis, appear to be nonsense words. What is maximum? Or even worse, doesn't optimum mean something like perfection? Isn't it something we should try to approach rather than achieve?

Also potentially damaging to shareholder relationships is anything that smacks of "pop" or "faddish" language. Here again, Winston Churchill had something to say on this important subject. When he was the leader of the Loyal Opposition after World War II, he soon found that the thing most obnoxious "to his mind" in socialist planning was their jargon. The poor became the "lower income disadvantaged."

Churchill bitterly reacted to this as he did to their description of a house as a "local accommodation unit." He announced to the entire House of Commons: "Now we will have to change that favorite old song, 'Home Sweet Home', to say 'Local Accommodation Unit, Sweet, Local Accommodation Unit'—'There's No Place Like Local Accommodation Unit.'"

Simple direct language really helps improve communication. Don't use phrases like (this is an actual example) "We will institute implementation of these projects on an accelerating basis." The project was late getting started; they intended to start it at a later date;

therefore, couldn't they have just used a one-syllable word in place of twenty syllables, namely the work "start"?

Another example is, "Financial instability in major financial institutions can cause significant externalities in the form of systematic disruptions." Apparently the writer was saying something along the lines of, "If there are a lot of bank failures this could be bad for the economy." Dr. Maryann Jennings of Arizona State University reported in an excellent op-ed in the Wall Street Journal, quoting an actual memo of the type that often finds itself in shareholder communications, "In macroeconomics we rely heavily on optimization—specifically: maximizing utility subject to a production possibilities frontier and subject to a budget constraint." What does it mean? According to Dr. Jennings, it wasn't so much a matter of what the writer meant. She wrote that the more relevant question was, "Who cares?"

It is also apparent that shareholders do not want the opposite treatment either; to be treated as children. Some annual reports appear to be written for the ten-year-old, with lots of pictures and a lack of words, particularly long ones. Somewhere in between the two extremes is the most effective.

Consistency And Change
As in dealing with any group of people, one of the biggest challenges in shareholder relationships is how to explain and reconcile the sometimes contradictory concepts of consistency and change. Tom Peters has been quoted as saying that, "People have two basic and equally strong needs—stability and change."

If by consistency he means, and I believe he does, commitment to certain underlying principles; commitment to shareholders, customers, employees; commitment to staying competitive; commitment to innovation; commitment to good corporate citizenship, then he makes good sense. Consistency is popular with shareholders, possibly even a requirement.

At the same time, shareholders, as Tom Peters says, want change. They want their company to be able to respond to changes in domestic and international markets; they want them to be able to respond, and quickly, to new opportunities and new technologies. They also want them to be able to change and respond to different, and often new, customers needs and wants.

Full Disclosure And Bad News

One of the most important parts of securities law in the United States comes under what the lawyers call "full disclosure." Fortunately this tough part of the law is very ethical. All it says is that information that is disclosed to one shareholder must be given to all shareholders. No shareholder is entitled to get a "head start" over others. This is what the media calls "insider information." Therefore to follow these laws is not as difficult as it might sound. It goes back to the Golden Rule. Treat people right. Build honest relationships with shareholders.

A common mistakes in shareholder relations is poorly disseminated bad news. Some companies simply cannot bear to let all the bad news out at once, so they dribble a little bit at a time. Even Machiavelli said don't do that. He said it is okay to give out good news a little bit at a time, but bad news should be given out all at once.

A company in the trucking business once bought a bank. A common joke was that pretty soon banks would be buying trucking business-es. As one would expect, the trucking company did well in trucking and poorly in banking. The shareholders got the bad news a little bit at a time over a period of a year or so.

The company was run by honest people. They weren't trying to cheat or mislead the shareholders. The problem was that it looked that way. There really was no malice or intent to mislead, but it cer-tainly gave that impression.

A more recent example would be the bad news that came out of Wall Street a little bit at a time about Drexel Burnham or, more recently, Kidder Peabody. It seems that the shareholders got a little bad news, then a week or two later more, and then a couple of weeks later, a little more. This was not well received. Both companies, who at one time were strong, no longer exist.

A Note On Ethics
Much is now being written about business ethics. Colleges now include it in their curriculum. Dr. Maryann Jennings, a business pro-fessor at Arizona State University, now directs the Lincoln Center for Applied Ethics at Arizona State. In many op-eds and other writ-ings, she has made a lot of sense concerning the very difficult and involved subject of business ethics. She has written, "We have equated certain social goals with business ethics. While we may

wish to believe that commitment to social issues is a good measure of ethical conduct, it is not an absolute determinant of fairness and honesty." She then asks a provocative question, "Is commitment to the rain forest as important as truth in labeling?" or "Is animal testing as critical as fair and honest treatment of franchisees?"

But then she says something I don't agree with. She says, when referring to the exercise of business ethics, "No one is checking." *Au contraire.* Shareholders check regularly on the companies in which they invest. Warren Buffett would agree. Also customers check, as well as suppliers and employees. When they see a lack of ethics, this damages otherwise good relationships. If they see a pattern of poor ethics continuing, they have the right to, and often do, end these relationships.

Shareholder Activism

A recent development in shareholder relations is, in the opinion of many, very encouraging. This trend is what is known as shareholder activism. Companies with good relations with shareholders will welcome this trend.

One of the best examples of this occured a few years ago when a man named Bob Monks tried to get himself voted onto the board of Sears. He said, apparently sincerely, that he didn't really want board representation, but he wanted the company to go back to what they had been successful at, namely retailing. He asked them to quit being a "promiscuous conglomerate."

Many people thought he was like the man from LaMancha, but

within a year Sears sold its brokerage firm, Dean Witter Reynolds, and then the real estate firm, Coldwell Banker. Later they even sold a 19 percent stake in Allstate Insurance. About two years later, they spun off the other 81 percent of Allstate to the shareholders. This was one of the largest spin-offs in financial history, and it was aimed at turning the company back into a pure retailer. Most critics now agree that this benefitted shareholder value and it has proven to be popular with the shareholders.

This reminds me of a little dialogue I heard down on Wall Street one time when a big executive of a major corporation said to one of his associates, "What the hell do the shareholders know?" His associate said, "I don't know, but they own the place."

Annual Reports And Newsletters

Annual reports are one of the most important means for a company to communicate with its shareholders. Knowing this, it is amazing to note how carelessly put together many annual reports are. Some are excellent, some are fair, and some are just bad communications. Take out a stack of annual reports, glance through them quickly and ask yourself, after you have flipped through each report, "What does this company do?" and "How are they doing?" Three out of four don't tell you, maybe even more.

Also take a look at the chairman's or president's letter. Some are excellent, but some do nothing more than repeat the numbers that are already illustrated on the summary page and again in the complete financials further back in the report. Why simply repeat something that has been illustrated twice? How informative is that?

On the bright side, there are some excellent annual reports. Warren Buffett's Berkshire-Hathaway is considered to be possibly the very best. And for good reasons. His annual reports are things of beauty, full of interesting information, conveyed in a serious and at the same time entertaining manner. He tells not only how the company is doing but also why they are doing what they are doing.

Buffett explains technical subjects in simple yet interesting terms. One time he was explaining to shareholders why they were retaining an investment in a company that wasn't doing too well. He said, "We won't close down a business of sub-normal profitability just to add a fraction of a point to our corporate returns. I also feel it is inappropriate for even an exceptionally profitable company to fund an operation once it appears to have unending losses in prospect. Adam Smith would disagree with my first proposition and Karl Marx would disagree with my second; the middle ground is the only position that leaves me comfortable." Well said!

Tender Offers And Takeovers

The strengths of shareholder relationships are occasionally tested by tender offers. Basically there are two kinds of tender offers—friendly and unfriendly. Either type is a real test of the quality of the relationship between the company and the shareholders/owners.

Let's take the friendly offer first, since it is much more common. When the tenderer is told by the target that they are not looking for partners and are not in favor of selling out, one of the first things the tenderer, assuming they are experienced and sophisticated, does is to check on the quality of the relationships between the company and the shareholders/owners. If this relationship is strong, in most cases, the tenderer tends to back away. He realizes then that any offer only moderately above the market or known value would probably be rejected by the shareholders.

With strong relationships, particularly long-term strong relationships, shareholders are expecting (more than just hoping) and looking forward to future substantial gains. Therefore, an offer only moderately above present value would not sound too attractive. Conversely, if the relationship is shaky or, even worse, hostile, the owner/shareholder would tend to jump at any offer, even slightly above the agreed value. Knowing that, the tenderer would be much more likely to pursue the offer and possibly even convert it into an unfriendly tender.

Unfriendly tenders are a form of economic warfare. Fortunately, they are rather rare, but they appear to be more frequent than they are because the media consider them to be great stories, partly due to the fact that they are indeed a form of combat. Here again the past relationships of the company and shareholders have a great influence on the outcome of the battle.

The importance of good shareholder relationships in takeover struggles was clearly seen when Bendix was attempting to acquire Martin-Marietta. Martin-Marietta apparently had good shareholder relations and vigorously opposed the unfriendly tender from Bendix. They fought back hard. They exhibited a great deal of vigor, also ingenuity in how to fight back. Their defense even earned a new name—the PacMan defense. They were buying up the attacker's stock while the attacker was buying up theirs.

The majority of Martin-Marietta shareholders stayed behind the company and supported it whereas that was not true at Bendix. William Agee, the head of Bendix, who many said was a brilliant person, was apparently not on good terms with many of the shareholders.

The result was that Bendix is no longer an independent company. They ran to the "white knight" Allied Signal for protection. It strikes some people that the white knight/black knight concept is like avoiding being eaten by an unfriendly lion by becoming a meal for a friendly one. In any event, the company with strong shareholder relations remained independent, as they wished, and the other did not.

Boundarylessness
The concept of boundarylessness applies in very important ways to shareholder relations. One example that comes up frequently is the opportunity for a company to enhance and increase shareholder value by combining technologies. These opportunities are much more easily recognized and acted upon within the concept of boundarylessness unless walls continue to be built between different parts of the company.

The *Economist* of London, in its June 5, 1995, issue, addressed this in a very interesting way, without using the word or concept of boundarylessness. They wrote of the rapid change in technologies which often meant opportunities to "the winners" and problems to "the losers." They summed it up very well by saying, "The capacity to think across boundaries—to spot opportunities at the juncture of two or more industries ... is important to success in today's environment."

We had an example of this quite recently in our company when we developed the Smart Motor (a combination of an electric motor with electronics). The Smart Motor combines technologies which have historically been separate. In most companies these technologies are considered so diverse that a company produces only one or the other. Or if they produce both, they are designed and marketed by separate divisions.

When the concept of the Smart Motor became popular with customers, it was difficult to combine these two technologies when they were divided in the conventional way. Therefore, the concept of boundarylessness and the ability to combine technologies quickly and efficiently had the prospect to greatly increase shareholder value.

In addition, the ability to combine new technologies within one company or one part of a company often has quite synergistic effects. The old definition of two plus two equals five applies when different technologies later become compatible and are combinable.

Another advantage to the shareholder is that when the company is able to spot these opportunities to combine these new technologies, the company is able to avoid the trap of forced diversification. Diversifications are much riskier than augmentations, due to some obvious facts such as lack of familiarity with technologies and markets.

As with many other new concepts, boundarylessness is really an exercise of common sense. It often means knocking down walls and adding considerable shareholder value with new products, new markets, and new customers. It need not be costly. The company uses available resources and assets. It is just a matter of putting them together in new ways.

The word "division" used by many companies usually means exactly that. It means they are divided. Divisions are sometimes even hundreds or even thousands of miles apart. Often the people in one division don't even know the people in the other. If they know each other at all, they often think of them as competitors, rather than colleagues. Boundrylessness doesn't thrive with "profit centering" and divisionalization.

The profit center concept has solved some problems, but it has created more. It is often the antonym of boundarylessness. It promotes competition within the company rather than without. Also, many inequities, or certainly perceived inequities, appear.

The advantage of this type of management is ease of monitoring—keeping score. It is not the complete score, but it is simple. Simple, but wrong, because it only looks at part of the true picture—all left brain. It is also wrong because it puts profit ahead of relationships, rather than the opposite. This is not to the long-term advantage of the owners.

Conclusion

To sum up, shareholders want to make a profit. Also, shareholders want many of the same things that customers and employees want. They want to be treated fairly. They want to be told the truth. They want to be kept informed. They want success. They want to feel they are part of the team. They want to feel that they are on a winning team. They want to feel that they made a good decision in becoming an owner of the company.

ABOUT SUPPLIERS

Introduction

When I originally outlined this book, I was planning to stick with the premise that has stood us in good stead for many years. That is that the three key constituencies for any business, large or small, are their customers, employees and owners. The primary premise is that the goal for future success should be to build strong, good, long-lasting relationships with these three constituencies. A secondary premise is to work hard and continuously to balance among these these three relationships, not favoring one over either of the other two. Remember C-E-O!

I furthered this premise with the analogy of the three-legged stool; namely that the only way a three- legged stool can support its intended and designed burden is for all three legs to be strong enough to carry their share of the load. Weakness in one would eventually result in collapse of the stool. The analogy contends that this would mean failure for the entire enterprise.

However, several associates have encouraged me to include suppliers as a fourth key constituency. I resisted this. Although recognizing that suppliers are very important, I could not quite convince myself that they were as important as the customer, employee, and owner (shareholder) constituencies. Or possibly I was enamored by the three-legged stool.

I am coming around to agreeing with these associates for two reasons. First, due to their urging, and second, due to the fact that suppliers are indeed becoming more important than they were in the past.

There are two basic reasons for this increasing importance. First is the fact that the leisurely pace of the past is long gone. The business race now goes to the swift. Most successful organizations are working hard, and quite often successfully, to cut down the time they require to do everything. They are cutting down time to supply their customers (the critical dimension between the time the customer states his that need and need is filled), time to develop new products, and time to improve old ones. Time to do everything is rapidly become foreshortened.

There are lots of buzzwords for this. The most popular is JIT, just in time. I am not going to use this phrase because it means many different things to different people. But its meaning has two important elements across all groups. These are speed and closer relationships between buyers and suppliers. To do this, they need closer relationships.

The second reason that suppliers are becoming more important is that there is a basic trend to have fewer and fewer suppliers. Several factors are given for this. Probably the most basic one is that with fewer suppliers it is easier to build truly strong and long-lasting relationships. Previously, suppliers were often thought of as adversaries by customers, and were treated as such. Relationships were often strained and many times short-lived.

This change, and it is obviously a healthy one in terms of building strong relationships, has happened and is happening. Therefore, I have swallowed my pride, at least partially, and I am now willing to consider suppliers as a key constituency. Possibly we could speak of a four-legged stool?

Some time ago the *Wall Street Journal* contained a very interesting full-page advertisement by Xerox. Rather than advertising some Xerox product or promoting their company's capabilities, this advertisement was entitled "Congratulations to our Xerox Certified Suppliers."

It then listed about 200 suppliers who had met their requirements to be certified. They referred to them as "an elite group" who had "teamed" with Xerox to provide world-class products. It said: "With us they believe that continuous involvement between customers and suppliers is the best way to achieve the highest quality." Would Xerox or anyone else have run such a full-page ad several years ago?

Most of us took a long time to learn that suppliers are very important people. Of course, we knew they were important when we needed their steel or aluminum and we had to have it, but we didn't think these relationships were as important as those with customers, employees, and shareholders.

This, though we didn't realize it at the time, often got us into strange and sometimes uncomfortable situations. For example, about 20 years ago our company was growing rapidly and had an increased need for cast iron. At that time most of the cast-iron foundries in the

United States were busy and were not accepting new customers. If they had, they couldn't have served them. We had good relationships with some small foundries, but they couldn't keep up with our growing needs. Therefore we either had to accept the situation as it was, which would definitely have stunted our growth (and strained good relationships with many of our good customers), or we had to find some way out of the situation.

In desperation we decided we would rent a plane (we were too small and poor at that time to have our own) and travel around the middle of the United States looking for a foundry that would accept some of our patterns and take care of part of our requirements. It began to dawn on us that part of our problem was that our purchasing department had concentrated more on numbers than relationships. Looking back, they weren't too good with the numbers either, but have improved greatly since.

We got five prospects, so we took off and visited these five foundries. Two of them turned us down cold. The next two told us about all of their problems in even taking care of the business they had already. After listening to all of their problems we decided they had more than we did.

So there we were, two days out, our ears full of foundry sand and rejections. Only one more call to make. This was on a small foundry in Indiana.

They turned out to be really fine people. Never met more honest, straightforward people. They knew what they were doing, understood their business, and were proud to be in it. The problem was that they, like others, were "booked up."

They began to get the drift that we were looking for a good long-term relationship, as well as cast iron. We asked several questions along these lines. We asked about their long-term plans for expansion. They had some interesting plans. We asked then if they weren't looking for some long-term customers to justify the need for this expansion. We pointed out that the foundry business was cyclical and that we were looking for a steady long-term supplier. Also, we showed them our impressive growth record. This interested them.

They were still saying no to us when lunchtime arrived. Since this was our last stop, and since we had the feeling of near panic that fishermen often get when they have no fish in the boat and the day is waning, we hung in there as best we could. After lunch, as we were getting better acquainted, they gave us a tour of their foundry. The equipment was not impressive, but the people were.

Later in the afternoon, as a storm was approaching, the foundry boss said he was worried about our flying out in such bad weather in a small plane. We said that we would like to get something settled before we left. He then agreed to take a couple of our patterns and see what he could do without promising any large quantities. He was thinking long term—the only one of the five that we had visited.

That was 20 years ago. That foundry has been one of our company's best suppliers ever since. Our relationship is now extremely strong. It took several years to become so, and now it is among the strongest of any of our suppliers. This has been good for both of our companies. Since that time there have been other periods of shortages of cast iron. Also, there have been periods of time when foundries needed business to keep their doors open. There were times when they badly needed us. We are now their largest and best customer and have been year after year.

That experience and that relationship had to do with supply and demand. Other strong relationships are built around technology and joint research and development. Although it seems obvious that suppliers should offer to customers all the research and development assistance possible, it doesn't always work that way.

One of the most common hurdles is one we engineers don't want to admit. That is the old NIH (Not Invented Here) syndrome. Many other things have changed, but NIH has been with us forever. It probably goes back to the Greeks, Romans, and Phoenicians. In other words, if it isn't our engineering development, it is not as good as ours is (or will be or could be.)

Here is another place where strong relationships are vitally important. Many suppliers have specialized laboratories that, for their specific type of products, are far superior to those of the customers. For instance a ball bearing manufacturer should, and usually does, have better facilities for testing bearings and developing better ones than any customer has.

They are usually eager to help. The supplier, unless he is a complete failure, sees the increasing importance of differentiating himself from other suppliers. This is of course a good way of doing it. Doing it, however, is easier said than done.

For example, several years ago we found that there was a type of insulation on the market that could considerably improve our products. The problem was that this special type of insulation was much more expensive than the conventional insulation that we had been buying for years. If it had only been slightly more expensive, we would have adopted it immediately. But it was far more expensive.

Having a good relationship at the time with one of the companies manufacturing this special insulation, we asked why it should be so much more expensive and wasn't there something that could be done about this. We were given lots of scientific reasons why it had to be more expensive.

After listening to all the science, chemistry, and engineering, it pretty much boiled down to the fact that since it was so high priced it was sold only in small quantities, so it was manufactured in small quantities. Therefore, we asked the obvious question: "If you manufactured this in large quantities, couldn't you produce it at only slightly higher cost than standard or conventional insulation.

We, of course, (I say of course because we had heard it so many times) received the conventional answer that it needed to be expensive because volume was so low and that it would always be that expensive because volume would always be that low. Our rejoinder was that if it were not so expensive, the volume could be high. We ended up in one of those chicken-and-egg discussions. This would have probably gone on for years as an impasse except for the fact that we did have a very good relationship with this company.

One day to the president of this company I brought up the question again; namely, why couldn't he just build a new factory specifically to make this new insulation? With the dedicated factory and larger quantities, the costs could become reasonable for both our companies and both would come out winners.

He then looked me in the eye and said, "Well, the only way we could afford to do this and convince our board of directors would be if we had a major customer commit to buy large quantities of this product." We said we could do that if the price were only slightly higher than the standard. The deal was made.

This turned out to be so successful that this arrangement has lasted for many, many years. In fact, it was later copied by other companies. In the meantime, and for a considerable length of time, they as the supplier had a head start on their competitors and we as the customer had a head start on ours. Without a good relationship, this could not have happened.

What Makes A Good Supplier Relationship?
1. Win-Win
As the two previous experiences illustrate, it is vitally important in building good long term relationships that both parties come out "winners." The old horse trading type of negotiations ended up with a winner and a loser. It usually didn't last very long. Some companies go from pillar to post trying out new suppliers yearly or even

more frequently. More and more this type of company that always tries to be on the winning side has difficulty finding good long-term supplier relationships. Some people, and this is certainly old-fashioned thinking, can't get it out of their heads that it is a zero-sum game, and that for them to win someone has to lose. This just ain't so! Win-wins are possible in most situations. They usually take more thought and knowledge to form. True, more time is needed in the beginning, but that time is saved many times during the life of the resulting good long-term relationship.

2. Learning From Each Other

A man at one of the smartest and most successful of our suppliers once told me that they "pick customers from what you can learn — what they bring to you in the way of knowledge." I asked him if he didn't think it worked both ways and he said it did. This is part of the win-win philosophy. It has been our experience that many innovations are actually combinations of ideas from both sides of the table.

The expression "both sides of the table" just used is pretty old-fashioned in itself. In the old days it was literally true. One party, supplier, or customer, lined up his troops on one side of the table while the others lined up on the opposite side. Then the crossfire began. Or as one of my mentors used to say, "Now the fight begins." It is difficult to believe how much negotiation methods have changed since that time. In those days most negotiations consisted of trying to best or beat each other rather than attempting to decide how we could help each other.

Some of those long combative type negotiations got amusing. For example, one time we were negotiating with a very tough customer and his right-hand man. He was a pretty tough guy also. We started out at about midmorning with me and my associate on one side of the table and the customers on the other side. The president of that company was beating us up pretty badly. I noticed as the day progressed that my associate was gradually inching his chair around toward the other side of the table. By lunchtime he was about in no man's land and after lunch he was slightly around on the customer's side.

I wasn't sure whether this tough customer had a sense of humor or not. One way to find out was to try. So I told the boss by about midafternoon that I thought these were very unfair negotiations. He asked me what I meant. I replied that it was three against one. I was mighty pleased when he laughed. From that moment on, we started thinking together and worked together. We've now done this very successfully for 20 years. We learned a lot from these people about their technologies in a very specialized industry, and I think they learned from us about the use of motors and which type of motors fit which types of applications. Actually this turned out to be a competitive advantage for them which they used quite skillfully.

3. Strong Reputations
Fortune recently ran its annual survey of the most and least admired companies. One thing that came through clearly this year was the increasing belief that reputation will grow in value as an important asset. As we have been noting, many companies are shrinking their number of suppliers, many quite drastically. This is done, or should

be done, with the hope and plan of forging stronger ties with those who make the cut. Reputation is bound to be increasingly important.

Fortune reports that it appears to many of these CEOs of most admired companies that the aureole, the reputation, around the company becomes all the more important as an introduction and as a basis for building strong relationships.

A difficult thing about discussing reputation is that this important word means different things to different people. In common, however, are meanings such as trust, integrity, reliability, and "ones we have faith in." From a practical point of view, it is often stated as "If we have trouble with a product or service, will the supplier stand behind it?" Or as the far and away best-selling book ever written says, "Faith is the belief in the unseen." Of course, reputation is unseen. A brilliant man once told me, "People who can see what other people don't see, often the most important things in life, are rare."

Another reason good reputations are so valuable is that they take a long time to mature; in part due to the length of time needed to prove integrity. As one great educator once said when asked to graduate a brilliant student in two years, "It takes four years to grow a good college graduate." When challenged, he continued, "It takes two years to grow zucchini. Which do you want?"

4. Desire
As we see in sports frequently, sometimes the little guy with a little less talent wins the big game anyway. How could this be? It is

because of desire. The same with relationships with suppliers.

When IBM was in its heyday ten or fifteen years ago, they had great resources, probably more than all their competitors put together. These resources included not only a tremendous amount of net worth, but also a huge organization, a strong sales and service group, a complete line of products, and more money to spend on research and development than the entire revenue of most of their competitors. But as years went by it became more and more apparent that they had begun to rest on their laurels, whereas some of their competitors were trying very hard to get even a small part of the computer market.

Then to speed this change in leadership, which came along pretty fast in the '90s, arrogance started creeping in. Actually, it charged in at IBM during the '70s and '80s. Feelings of arrogance create exactly the opposite effect on customers as does desire. It turns off good relationships rather than building them.

To sum up, if all other things are equal or even near equal, the winner is often the one who wants to win the most.

5. Ideas and Creativity
Another thing customers look for when selecting a supplier for a long-term relationship is ideas. If quality, price, delivery and other aspects of the product or service, are comparable, the supplier with good ideas for the customer will end up on top. Good ideas are certainly powerful and valuable. A major factor of success as a continuing stream of good ideas.

Until recently, most supplier rating systems did not take this into consideration. Most were strictly numerical indices based on simple formulas for price, on-time delivery and other measurable factors. Since ideas, reputation, integrity, responsiveness, and many other important factors are not quantifiable, they were often left out of the ratings. Many customers have now seen the error of their ways and are adding these factors into ratings of their suppliers.

6. Value

This is the sum of what customers look for in their suppliers. An example of how to evaluate value is discussed as the Baldor Value Formula. This was developed 20 years ago for sales training. Back in the days when the customer and the supplier were still adversaries, the new salesman was often "beaten up" when he first went out solo. The most common way for this to happen was for the customer to put a big emphasis on price: "You're not competitive on price; go back and get me another quote." This left the neophyte salesman in a difficult position, as he didn't know how to respond. As one young salesman told me, "Before I knew it, I was out in the parking lot."

Another valuable use for this formula is in evaluating suppliers. It shows four independent variables adding up to value. Value is what people really buy, not price or quality or any one of the four variables. Also, the formula contends that the four factors are of equal value. Therefore, the "price" argument is intellectually and practically flawed since it only considers one of the four variables.

The idea in developing this formula was, first, to help a new salesman to learn for himself that the four variables were important and, second, to be able to present this to his customer. This allowed him to present a more well-rounded agenda and encouraged him to ask questions of the customer as we wanted him to do so that he could learn what was needed and wanted from the customer's perspective. As he learned more about the customer he was better able to fit his product to what the customer needed with increasing success. He was able to become a better supplier.

Conclusion

In their excellent 1995 Annual Report, Chrysler Corporation included suppliers as an important group along with shareholders, customers, and employees. They said that, in effect, to do the best job for shareholders, good relationships with these other three groups were needed. Chrysler described an ongoing supplier-company program to improve quality, lead time, scrap and other factors as being very successful. In one year this included 63 production workshops with 25 leading suppliers.

The word "partners" is being used more and more to describe supplier-company relationships. As more effort to work together in a win-win way is expended, the more true this becomes.

We recently had a very gratifying example of the importance of good relationships with suppliers. We had designed a new type of motor part that required a large amount of cooperation between us and the supplier of a vital component. We later found that a competitor of ours had approached this supplier to make this component for them. This would have been a loss to us of an important competitive advantage.

What happened? Our supplier said, "This was Baldor's idea." And the supplier would not duplicate it for our competitor. They also said, "Our relationship goes way back and we have no intention of damaging this good relationship." It was very gratifying to see that this supplier used the word "relationship" twice in a direct quote.

To sum up, I am now considering that the four-legged stool rather than a three-legged stool is an appropriate analogy. Suppliers are an important constituency and becoming more important all the time.

EPILOGUE

This book lays out a philosophy for managing a company, large or small. This is the philosophy which has guided us here at Baldor for many years. Although I can't guarantee that you will be successful if you follow this philosophy, I can tell you that it has worked for us. Baldor has built strong relationships with customers, employees and shareholders, with profitable results. During the last 10 years, we have more than quadrupled our earnings and almost tripled our sales. With each of our three constituencies we can point to real success because of strong relationships.

In 1997 Baldor was the first choice in the industrial motor field by customers in 83 percent (15 of 18) of all known customer preference surveys. We are proud of this.

We continue to have a strong relationship with our employees. Confirmation of this has come to us often in many ways. In the January 12, 1998, issue of *Fortune*, Baldor was named one of the "100 Best Companies To Work For In America."

For shareholders total return in the last 10 years has been almost 500 percent. This kind of return strengthens relationships with shareholders.

Although many continue to think the purpose of a business is first and foremost to make money, other perspectives exist. Peter Drucker wrote that the purpose of a business is to "create customers." In Michael Novack's excellent book, *Business As A Calling*, David Packard of Hewlett-Packard is quoted as explaining why a company exists in the first place: "Why are we here? I think many people assume, wrongly, that a company exists solely to make money." Novack says that making money is "an important result of a company's existence, if the company is any good." But he says, "A result is not a cause."

These thoughts are important to me, and I hope to you. One reason is a very practical one — namely that companies, and their leaders, who think this way and really believe usually make more money than those who don't. Hewlett-Packard is certainly a good example. Remember, relationships first and success follows.

An important subjective reason is that working, while thinking of doing a good job for other people, is more fun. And doing a good job for other people—employees, customers, and owners—makes for a really good three-legged stool.